Mastering Life's Adventures:
On the Beam

Wheel graphics designed by Greg Fawcett

Visit Dr. Holder's book website for free download of *Mastering Life's Adventures: On the Beam* wheel graphics: http://www.masteringlifesadventures.com

Mastering Life's Adventures:

On the Beam

Dear Steve,

It has been a pleasure to be in your presence and the warmth of your soul. May you continue to "stay on the Beam!"

Peace and Love,
Judith
9-22-2012

Judith C. Holder, Ph.D.

Dedication

This book is dedicated to people from every walk of life searching for something more meaningful and deeper, and for ways to apply spiritual principles in their daily lives. This book is dedicated to your Soul and in gratitude to those who have sponsored mine.

Acknowledgements

Many seen and unseen people have informed my way of thinking and served as an inspiration for writing this book. I acknowledge God and all His influences in my exploration and soul growth. I thank my parents (my mother passed in 2003) and their quest for Truth, which influenced my knowledge about soul evolution and the deeper meaning of life. I give an endearing appreciation to Elizabeth Clare Prophet (1939 – 2009), who was before her time, a teacher of Truth among us. Her discourses and great love of the souls of men and women has been an inspiration to understanding spiritual principles for everyday life. She opened a door to my divine understanding and knowledge of the Ascended Masters, universal Christ consciousness and teachings on the relationship between God, karma, dharma, reincarnation and the soul's advancement on this planet.

My gratitude flows to my family for their ongoing love and encouragement. I also would like to thank Peggy Neuman and Harvey Harbrough for their editorial support, and Margaret Paul, Ph.D., for her helpful manuscript suggestions. I especially thank all the unseen heavenly host hands that have guided me throughout my life and continue to do so.

Contents

Foreword

In my first meeting with Dr. Judith Holder, I was immediately struck with her sense of presence, warmth, openness and serenity. As I spent time with her and got to know her, and experienced the depth of her devotion to being an instrument of God's love on the planet, I could readily see why she so beautifully embodies these qualities.

One of the things that has always been very important to me is to know that an author is walking her talk. There is no doubt that this is true with Dr. Holder. Her devotion to learning and loving is truly awesome, and she brings this depth of commitment to "Mastering Life's Adventures: On the Beam." This is not a book of intellectual knowledge, but a book of deep knowing that comes from Dr. Holder's direct experiences in working with herself and with others.

For anyone on a spiritual path, this book is must reading. I do not believe you can read this book without being inspired to consciously embrace more and more of the "Twelve Constructive Qualities of the Soul." Judith simply and clearly helps you see the difference between being governed by your 'ego-persona' and your soul's desire for oneness with God.

Most of us don't consciously think about what our soul needs on a daily basis to feel peaceful and fulfilled. As Judith points out, many people spend their lives hungry for *something,* but they don't know what the 'something' is. Instead, they turn to various addictions to try fill their emptiness, not understanding that it can be filled only with the love that is God. But the love that fills us cannot flow through us when we close our hearts with any of "The Twelve Diminishing Aspects of the Soul," – our programmed behaviors from our ego-persona.

This beautiful little book is about tending to what your soul truly wants and needs, rather than what your ego wants and thinks it needs. It is a book that will help you contemplate who you are and why you are here on the planet.

I feel privileged to write the Foreword for this little book. I hope all of you receive as much benefit from it as I have.

Blessings on your healing journey,

Margaret Paul, Ph.D.
Author, *Do I Have To Give Up Me to Be Loved by God?*

October 2011

Introduction
Is there a deeper meaning to life?

It is five o'clock in the morning. You are startled, awakened from a deep sleep by your two-year-old daughter, fussily crying for your attention, while simultaneously your alarm blares in your ear. In one not so graceful movement, you reach to turn off the annoying alarm while jumping up to attend to your child. Your heart is racing. Beneath its loud beating, you sigh and mumble, "Well, here goes another day."

Of course, you love your baby and your family, but you are finding it increasingly challenging to maintain your hectic life. You feel as if you are on a twenty-one speed Olympic bike racing to keep up with all of the demands.

Your challenges are expanding, the days are long, the job meetings are tiring, your patience with your partner is growing thin, and your nerves are often on edge.

When you are finally still and quiet, you experience a sinking sensation that turns into feelings of irritability and even despair. This is when you think, *there must be something more to life than this.*

So you try the various fads in an attempt to reduce your stress—reflection, jogging, going to the gym, outings in the wilderness, taking mental health days from work—but none of these seem to quiet the racing discontentment of your thoughts, nor lessen the pull of partner, children, job, and other obligations. You try hard to keep the sinking feeling at bay, but it lingers and even increases. Sometimes it is all you can do just to hold on to your pseudo-surface calmness.

Then, one late night while you're reading to your two-year-old night owl, a light bulb turns on in your mind. As your baby drifts off to sleep, you think about the numerous self-help books that are available: the how-to's for developing social skills, problem-solving skills, succeeding in life, and bettering oneself. You realize that you have not come across a book specifically written for the spiritually minded on *spiritual life skills*.

And so, you think about the book you would love to find that would give you the answers to your questions: "How do I use daily, practical spiritual skills and principles to root myself in my spiritual identity that could bring a greater, more satisfying and rewarding sense of direction, purpose and service to my life and others? And just what are these skills?"

You would love a book that is not directed toward formal religious doctrine, one that is not solely based on Catholicism, Buddhism, Judaism, Christian-ism, etc. Rather, it would be one that is universal, that is easily read and understood, and that imparts practical and useful spiritual information.

If this sounds like you and your life challenges, then this is the book for you. Whether or not you attend a denominational or non-denominational church or consider yourself independently spiritual, this book focuses on the essential keys, principles and spiritual skills necessary to live a more complete and fulfilling life.

Just as you can learn skills to increase your grace in speaking, displaying etiquette at the table, communicating effectively with others, and interacting in social gatherings, you can learn spiritual skills that will help you evolve along the spiritual journey of your life.

These are the skills you can apply in all phases of your life, from singlehood to child rearing, to family life or personal and professional relationships, to work or retirement. These are the skills you will use to reconnect with your core—your essential self, the real, authentic YOU!

PART I

Principles for Mastering Life's Adventures

Everything that limits us, we have to put aside.
~ Jonathan Livingston Seagull

Chapter 1

Outer Versus Inner Realities:
The Twelve Qualities of the Soul

I have no special revelation of God's will. My firm belief is that He reveals himself daily to every human being, but we shut our ears to the "still, small voice."
~ Gandhi

We seem to come into this life with little awareness of what life is all about. We do the things most people do, those things we are expected to do. When we try to scratch the surface to see whether there is a deeper meaning to life, we run into dead ends, thinking the day-to-day grind is what it's all about. But there continues a gnawing feeling that will not stop brothering us. It is like an inner prompt that's never quiet for very long. It is during those still, quiet times in our life that we might experience a deep yearning for more meaning, more direction, more understanding and more appreciation.

Maybe there is a reason for this prompting. Just maybe at our core there lies our essential real self, longing for expression. This is the part in us that is divine, attempting to live in this material, external world of events, experiences, things, and pseudo-glamour.

I believe our spirit-spark, which I like to refer to as our "soul" or "essential self", needs the space to blossom. It is this inner urge to bloom that keeps us dissatisfied and searching for something more in life. It is our soul, our essential real self, that is prompting us to look for something more. It longs for a sense of connection to something greater than the smallness of our outer selves and our exterior lives.

As Jane, a 22-year-old attending college, states, "I have this urge to do something." She frequently feels an inner yearning for something more. She thinks it might be restlessness with being in school. She considers herself an extrovert and active. She goes to class, attends parties, goes on dates and gets decent grades, and she hopes to graduate in two years. She has a small group of friends, and they comment on how much fun she is to be around. Jane engages in many activities, but she still doesn't feel inner contentment.

Then there is Danielle, a second year graduate student in college, and Davis, who is in his mid-thirties. Both notice they are gaining a significant amount of weight, and they mistake the inner urge of restlessness as an urge to eat. Both engage in emotional eating to fill the inner void, which brings only temporary relief. The urge, the gnawing feeling, eventually comes back. They feel not only restless, but disgusted about their weight gain as well.

The void is interpreted by the personality as a physical need, but the urge may be coming directly from our soul. There is a difference between the soul and the personality. The personality is finite and is the mask we show the outer world. The soul is that spark of divinity that exists within us, that knows far more than the personality mask of self. We do not always know how to tap into the soul (essential self) or unearth the specialness of who we are. Our soul, through promptings, attempts to bring its existence to the attention of our outer self.

When we finally come to realize that our first spiritual life skill is to pay attention to the *inner promptings* for something deeper, something more transcendent than the human elements of self, we begin to walk the spiritual path. This is the path of understanding and honoring the needs of our soul, our essential self. Have you ever thought - *does my soul, my essential self, have specific needs?*

I have come to recognize the Twelve Constructive Qualities that build and expand the soul, leading to the unfolding of the soul and growth. You can think of these qualities as individual spokes on a wheel: the soul is the hub and the twelve spokes enable the wheel to turn, move forward, or spin at an appropriate frequency. As I touch upon these Twelve Qualities, see which ones resonate within you. We can use these soul qualities for expression and develop-ment throughout our entire life.

The Twelve Constructive Qualities of the Soul: The Interior Castle

1. Harmony
2. Gratitude (Appreciation)
3. Equanimity
4. Authenticity
5. Vision
6. Victory (Success)
7. Empowerment
8. Kindness (Affection)
9. Mastery
10. Self-Discipline
11. Obedience
12. Wisdom

The soul is derailed from the path every time these qualities are neglected or forgotten. The focus is then on the wants of the persona (personality), our outer self, the part we show to the world. You might never have thought of your soul as having desires, needs and a spiritual path to follow, but it does.

Each person on this planet has a soul, but many do not give it much thought because of the wants and desires of our personality, our ego. Ego is our *"Energy Going Out"* instead of the *substance of our life (soul)* moving inward. Our soul is light, love and truth. Our soul desires to love and be loved and be loving. Our soul, when given the opportunity, automatically feels connected to our essential source of energy, GOD.

This is what nourishes us, feeds us, and fills us up, like manna from heaven. Our soul longs for connection. Through this nourishing process, the indwelling of peace, and the continuous lifelong development of the Twelve Constructive Qualities, our soul expands and the personality-ego decreases, becoming subservient to the soul. The soul, then, becomes the ruler of our body temple, instead of the other way around.

Jeff came to my office for executive coaching. He was smart, energetic, driven, and dogmatic, and he felt lost about why others found him intimidating and irritating. He had learned the way to get ahead was to remain focused on his goal, which was to increase revenue for his company.

Jeff was disconnected from the emotional part of his nature. He felt that emotions did not matter; however, he was very anxious, angry and critical of himself and others. He had little awareness of how much his ego was ruling and smothering his soul sensitivities, and his desire for harmony and success. Only after I questioned him and gave him some self-reflective exercises did he begin to see clearly how his ego was ruling him and that the best parts of himself were becoming more and more dormant. His ego desire for material success at all costs to self and others was creating havoc in his life and in his relationships.

Those around him saw a middle-aged man (his external mask) who was bent on succeeding at someone else's expense, was inflexible in his approach, and became easily irritated with the people around him. During the coaching session, Jeff chose three soul qualities (harmony, appreciation, authenticity) to cultivate in himself and in his interactions with people around him. After several months of integrating these qualities into his thinking, feeling, and interactions, Jeff reported feeling grounded, having more energy (reduction in his stress level), and receiving positive feedback from colleagues. He also found that he was still meeting his profit margins for the business. He was truly amazed and was eager to learn about his soul psychology.

Finding ways in which we can infuse these Twelve Constructive Qualities into our daily living by examining our daily thoughts, feelings and behaviors, enables us to be more Christ-like[1] thereby expressing more of our divinity.

When we infuse our soul with these constructive qualities, the wheel begins to spin and develop a momentum, oscillating at a higher frequency, which bursts into a marvelous spark of light! This is who we really are! We are light beings! We are spiritual beings here on Planet

Earth to show forth our light as light bearers. That is pretty astounding. Just think, if we can get past our ego-persona, we can transcend the ugly duckling and become the swan of natural grace and beauty.

Grace, a mother of three young children, had a husband who cherished her. She decided that she wanted to cultivate soul growth. She was tired of screaming at her children for messing up every room in the house and nagging her husband to come home early to help with the kids. This daily hassle resulted in Grace feeling angry, resentful and very moody. During a coaching session, she said, "I really want to be different but I don't know how to do it. I feel like I'm stuck in a rut."

We talked about what soul qualities she wanted to develop after she discussed what was important to her in life, her personal values and her vision of who she wanted to be in a year's time. From that conversation, she decided to start with two constructive soul qualities, Harmony and Authenticity. We discussed what these qualities would look like in her life, what she needed to let go of in order to cultivate these qualities and what situations and events could derail her success. Once she gained some momentum with cultivating these qualities in her interactions with husband and family, she added working on holding the immaculate "Vision" and "Kindness." Pleased with the results, Grace said things that use to bother her no longer did, and she could see changes in her attitude, thoughts, and behavior toward her family.

It is helpful to start small by working on two to three qualities at a time. That way we can gain momentum and a consistency in transforming the thinking, feeling and behavioral patterns that cause discomfort. Grace realized that the approach she was taking with her children and husband was not working. All she felt on a daily basis was anger, frustration, irritability and sadness. This was not pleasant for her, the kids or husband.

Grace and I discussed her mindset, her beliefs about what it meant to be a mother and partner, before she began working on the soul quality of Harmony and Authenticity. As she began actively applying these qualities in her daily affairs, she found coaching very helpful in assisting with refining how she engaged with her family. She let go of trying to rigidly control her loved ones, and she developed more effective ways to interact with her children and husband. She felt a greater measure of inner peace, attunement and alignment with her soul, and a sense of direction and purpose.

Just as there are Twelve Constructive Qualities that fuel and uplift the soul, there are also Twelve Diminishing Aspects that rust over, weigh down and disempower the soul. Visualize the soul as becoming corroded, caked over, or burdened with the persona or ego (*energy going out*) shrouding the real or "essential" self.

Twelve Diminishing Aspects of the Soul

1. Indecision
2. Ingratitude
3. Worry
4. Dishonesty (Deception)
5. Resentment
6. Fear (Confusion)
7. Criticism
8. Anger (Hatred)
9. Doubt
10. Pride (Arrogance)
11. Rebellion (Disobedience)
12. Jealousy

We find ways to justify our thoughts, feelings and actions. Grace felt her kids and husband were being inconsiderate, and that provided justification for her resentment, anger and criticism. Whenever these destructive aspects are present, we are disconnected from our soul source, our divinity. Just as positive and negative attributes cannot occupy the same space, constructive qualities and diminishing aspects, cannot either.

You may be wondering, *how would these diminishing aspects manifest themselves in my life?* Or, *what would my ego-persona look like in my daily life?* I think a good response would be what Vanzant described in her book, *One Day My Soul Just Opened Up*[2]:

> "...continues to worry,
> lives in doubt,
> is afraid,
> judges other people,
> is afraid to trust,
> needs proof,
> believes only when it is convenient,
> fails to follow up,
> refuses to practice what it preaches,
> needs to be rescued,
> wants to be a victim,
> beats up on 'self,'
> needs to be right all of the time, and
> continues to hold on to what does not work..."

One of the reasons for our existence on this planet is to learn to become the positive, constructive attributes that uplift us, and to become the wheel that turns or spins at the frequency of light. Every time we manifest the constructive love qualities in our life, we build stronger ties with our inner self, our soul. The more we manifest the negative or diminishing traits in our life, the easier it becomes to disconnect from our source and live a life on the surface of self, in the outer world of effects.

Feeling disconnected, unplugged, and uncertain of our direction, and questioning the meaning of our life can make us feel like we are stagnant and drifting through life. When we do not have a drive or sense of deeper purpose, we begin to wonder what life is all about. Even if we haven't experienced these deleterious aspects ourselves, we know of other people around us who have experienced a sense of drifting. I know a mother whose 14-year-old daughter committed suicide because she couldn't get any "real" answers about why she was living. She preferred not to exist if there was no reason to be alive. This is a very sad, unfortunate, and all too common situation.

Fredric, an 18-year-old, is friendly. He likes to keep busy, and he easily becomes bored. He feels most alive when he's attending parties and is the center of attention. He likes to be the jokester, and when he is able to make friends and strangers laugh, he gets even sillier. When he is not being the center of attention, he is easily distracted at school and not performing up to his potential. He is actually pretty smart, but has gotten into the rut of just getting by. His parents are frustrated with him, and his short-fuse temper is the main reason he gets into fights with his peers and arguments with his teachers. It's just another way of getting an excitement fix in his otherwise boring routine.

On the other end of the life spectrum is Zita, an 85-year-old divorced woman in relatively good health, who spends most of her time thinking about a mixture of the "good times," and what she did not get from parents and friends, and watching TV. She loves all of the soaps on television. It is her way of retreating from feeling isolated and alienated from her family. Her three adult children are so busy that they rarely call or make contact with her. When she feels an urge to do something, she frequently shops during the day.

Both Fredric and Zita are living life the way they think it should be lived, the way they have seen others live, or have been taught through social customs, traditions and cultural mores. They may have had a desire for something more in life but looked around them and became involved in other less than fulfilling activities. They are doing what many are doing in life, just trying to get by and have a measure of fun or excitement along the way. They have a sense of restlessness and drifting through life, not sure of their direction or purpose. They misinterpret the urges they receive of wanting something more in their daily life as a need to shop, go to parties, watch television, etc.,. These activities are not necessarily bad—they have their appropriate place in our lives—but when they become constant distractors and conduits for energy *going out*, they become energy drainers.

The more our energy *goes out* into the world, the more we can be caught up in the day-to-day whirlwind of just making a living and getting by. Remember Jeff who was ego driven and disconnected from his inner self? He was critical, arrogant, and anxious. He needed to change his perspective.

It may seem counterintuitive, but the goal of life is like a figure-eight flow. There are times we need to be in the world, and there are times we need to flow back into a quiet place within ourselves and be still.

Energetic Flow of Life (External/Internal)

Our senses are continually bombarded with incessant noise from TV, commercials, blaring music, radios, nightclubs, chatting with others, and much more, all which keep our attention on our outer ego-personality. We get so involved in the external, outer world that we forget we need time to check in with our inner self. Our soul is literally starving for our attention.

This imbalance leads to our dissatisfaction, sadness, stress, restlessness, boredom and anxiety. As the saying goes, "Where we put our attention is where our experience will be."

Chapter 2

Our Attention
Informs Our Reality

*Authentic empowerment is the knowing that you
are on purpose, doing God's work, peacefully
and harmoniously.*
~ Wayne Dyer

I once heard that our attention is like a sunbeam shining through a magnifying glass. The intensity of the magnifying glass literally turns that ray into a flame, which burns the object of its attention. Attention is very powerful. It creates the things we want as well as the things that we do not want. We are the genies of our own lamps.

However, there is also a missing component to this attention perspective that we must take into consideration. What creates our reality is attention plus how we *feel* about a situation. In our Western world, we tend to look at the intellect as supreme and believe that all we have to do is think something into being. It's like a friend telling you that all you have to do is use a positive affirmation and say it twenty times and voila!.....you will get what you want. Well, for the majority of people, it does not happen like that.

That which creates our reality are the thoughts we *think*. These thoughts, wedded to the feelings we *feel*, create the momentum or spiral of energy, which then convert a positive or negative desire into manifestation. I think of *manifestation* as another word for *matter*. We have a lump of clay (matter) that is put on a potter's spinning wheel. Your right hand (thoughts) and left hand (feelings) are molding the clay into an object of your choosing. It takes many thousands of repetitions for an object (matter) to begin to take shape. What the final shape will look like is totally dependent upon the expertise of your hands, the qualitative attention of your thoughts and feelings.

Have you ever had a situation in which you felt that someone disrespected you, making a comment that was negative or demeaning? Even though you may not have spoken up at the time about how you felt, you found yourself thinking about the situation and reacting internally. You probably replayed the conversation over and repeatedly in your mind, maybe to the point that you couldn't fall asleep at night.

In the extremely early hours of the morning, you have these dialogues going on in your mind. You find yourself getting upset. Then you become angry and irritated and tell yourself that the next time you see the person, you are going too really let him or her know how you feel.

So, what are you molding from your thoughts and feelings? Anger? Frustration? Hurt? Despair? Sadness? Anxiety? On what are you focusing your attention? Remember, *attention equals thoughts plus feelings, which creates your reality*. A reality of negativity also has a negative influence on our physical health. You are engaged in intensifying the diminishing attributes, pushing you further away from your soul-attunement and creating ego-persona attachment. The more we are attached to our ego by being offended or worrying about what others think, the more we diminish the soul and let the ego-persona run rampant. The ego-persona believes it rules your castle.

Lucia was a terrific person but was frequently concerned about what others would think about her at work and at church. She frequently became anxious about what she was saying and worried about whether she might offend anyone. One day her anxiety became so intense, especially after giving a marketing healthcare presentation on an innovative approach to her colleagues and vice president, that she began having anxiety attacks. She went home and told her husband that she needed to go to the hospital because she couldn't breathe. Her heart was racing so fast that she felt it would come out of her chest. She felt like she was going to die. Her husband agreed to drive her to the hospital. The emergency department doctor checked out her symptoms and told her they might be caused by stress, worry, hyper-vigilance about others' opinions of her, and being overworked.

The spiritual life skill principle here is simply to be aware of where you are focusing your *attention*. Attention is the lever we use to pull or bring a "frequency-vibration of energy" into manifestation or reality.

Energy oscillates at different frequencies, or speeds, much like the molecules in our body. Molecules come together at different vibrational rates (or frequencies) to form our cells, tissues, arteries, organs, and bones, etc. Our body is similar to a magnificent orchestra, with all the different frequencies (e.g., cells, tissues, arteries, organs, bones) playing a magnificent sonata. They work harmoniously together, and they also create dissonance (dis-ease in our body). Remember the pottery analogy. We manifest a particular matrix through our thoughts and feelings.

Ask yourself the following questions: "How much time am I spending engrossed in negative dialogue or self-talk? How much time am I complaining about someone or something? How much time am I feeling angry or hurt by a situation?" Now go back to the Destructive Aspects wheel and fill in the percentage of time you engage in those twelve aspects. You might be surprised. We can spend a lot of our time and energy engrossed in downward-spiraling energy, being moody or irritable, or having "bad days." This only creates suboptimal living. What we have not owned up to is that we have created our reality by not being astute and discerning of how we are using our attention.

I had a client who stated that he, Joseph, now 61 years old and had not accomplished much in his life. He dwelled upon all the things that had not gone right, the bad choices he had made and his disappointing personal relationships. He also felt his parents were to blame for his not getting the love, support and financial assistance he needed when he was growing up, which resulted in his dropping out of college. His constant negative thinking (self-loathing) and reacting to his past experiences created an ongoing depressed mood, a constant state of feeling down and cynical about himself and life.

As James Allen stated quite well, "As a man thinketh, so is he." The universal principle is *attention (thoughts, feelings) plus repetition (how often we focus our attention on a situation or object) informs our reality*. Thus, our reality is *our reality*.

An example of this is Jean Forthright. She has worked hard in a small company in public relations for fifteen years. She exemplifies what her boss and company want in their employees. Over the past five years, however, Jean has seen several colleagues receive promotions, including a close co-worker. She wonders why this has not happened for her. Jean's creativity, ingenuity and productivity wane over the months, after her co-worker is promoted and becomes her new boss. She resents being overlooked for a promotion, and decides to submit her portfolio for promotion.

After several months of waiting to hear back, Jean learned that her promotion had been denied. Jean was devastated. She took action, speaking to her boss and to his superior, but she felt their responses were unhelpful.

She began having self-doubt, anxiety, anger and a general sense of injustice, all of which further affected her concentration and energy level. Jean's commitment and willingness to go the extra mile to get her projects completed began to fade. She found herself focusing on what management might be saying about her, how she felt used by the company and unappreciated for all her effort. She spiraled into nine months of negative, destructive thinking that affected her mood, health and work relationships.

Jean had gotten herself into a rut and became increasingly bitter. She decided to seek professional assistance to talk to about her feelings and concerns. With guidance, she began to make a course correction. Jean was able to turn her attention to, and focus on, what she *could* do, what was important to her in life (especially her relationship with her Higher Source, from whom she had been completely disconnected), and what she needed to surrender (e.g., resentment, anger, fear, doubt, anxiety) in order to make space for her faith. She realized that she was focusing her attention on the wrong things, and that she needed to remain focused on what was most important to her, the beneficial things in her life.

When Jean was willing to surrender the destructive, Diminishing Aspects and remain focused on the positive Constructive Qualities she brought to her job, she began feeling centered in her life. She felt grounded, even in the midst of this seeming injustice of not receiving a promotion, and ready for the future.

As she was able to consistently focus her attention (thoughts and feelings) on what she had control over and surrender her negative reactions, which derailed her connection with her soul-power, Jean began to turn the corner. She felt more balanced and empowered. Six months later, she received a promotion after she had let go of the desire for the promotion and re-focused herself on what she did best.

She realized that her negativity had been creating pain and disconnection from her inner soul-self. She knew she had to make some changes in her destructive thinking and feeling if she wanted to maintain her sense of integrity, and she did, with great results.

Jean happened to be sensitive to, and aware of, when she was *on the beam*. Picture yourself walking a balance beam. That beam is four inches wide (10 cm), with just enough room for a firm stance. It requires focused attention, a clear mind and heart, and determination to stay on the beam.

Can you see how this relates to life situations? We need to keep ourselves focused on what we want (staying on the beam) but flexible enough to maneuver to stay on the beam (centeredness). Centeredness is a quality of soul fulfillment. Be it a life situation in Jean's world or your world, you must realize that your reality is created by your attention, your feelings and your ability to remain positive, which keeps you connected to your soul power source.

So which Constructive Qualities on the soul qualities wheel would you like to use or cultivate to begin to keep anchored on the beam (see next page)?

Let us further explore the tug of war that sways us right or left, which can result in our falling off the beam and sometimes staying off the beam. As you know, falling off the beam because of distractions can be painful, just as in some of our life situations, encounters and decisions can keep us off the beam for short or extended periods of time.

The Twelve Constructive Qualities of the Soul

Chapter 3

Focus: Soul Quality
or Ego-Persona

*In the attitude of silence, the soul finds the path in
a clearer light, and what is elusive and deceptive
resolves itself into crystal clearness. Our life is a long
and arduous quest after Truth.*
~ Gandhi

Staying on the balance beam is no easy
feat, but it can be very rewarding and
fulfilling. It requires concentration,
practice and tenacity. It demands focus, a strong
mindset, dexterity and discipline. The tug of war
that we go through on a daily basis is about
keeping a spiritual soul-centeredness. It is about
how we stay centered in the midst of the
challenges in our daily routines. *Staying on the
beam* is the goal of your soul-spirit in the midst of
your problems, challenges, relationships and
situations.

You receive a call from your son's teacher.
He's misbehaving for the fourth time this week.
Your boss returns an assignment that you spent a
week preparing. She rips through it in 10 minutes,
hands it back with a disgruntled look, and tells you

it's not up to her standards. You receive a notice from the electric company informing you that they are turning off your service if you do not pay the balance by the end of the week. You come home to a spouse who is angry and argumentative because you are walking through the door at 8:00 p.m., tired and hungry, when you promised to be home by 6:00 p.m.

Anger, fear, doubt, worry, and anxiety are among some of the feelings you might be experiencing in these situations. These mood-states powerfully distract us from a spiritual-centered focus in our life. This can result in attending to *only* the daily grind (some might say, the hassles of living) without experiencing the goodness life can offer.

Our ego-persona thinks it's engaged in important activities because it's strategizing: how to get the son to behave, how to make the boss happy, how to keep the electricity on, and how to avoid an argument with the spouse—overall, how to get ahead in our affairs of daily living—but this does not necessarily lead to true happiness.

Of course, you have to focus your attention on resolving your daily life challenges. The real question you have to ask yourself is, "How am I handling these challenges? Am I overly engrossed in trying to handle my problems, losing sight of the spiritual significance for soul-growth in each experience in life? Am I engaged in the negative aspects of being annoyed, frustrated, and irritated because of the interruptions these problems create in my life? Do I find myself getting angry, becoming fearful and doubtful, and even nervous and worried? Do I find myself ruminating about my problems? Am I frequently interpreting many of my life experiences as negative and then overreacting?"

John, in his late-fifties, worked as a CPA in various firms for most of his professional career. He decided to quit his job due to ongoing frustrations with management and some of his co-workers. He started his own CPA business. He likes the fact that he sets his own schedule and decides which clients to take on. Clients find John very talented in his ability to find great tax breaks, but they dislike his rude behavior, critical, sarcastic comments and irritating gestures. When they do not provide him with tax materials in a certain format, he becomes irritated, sighs, points his finger and rolls his eyes. His customers feel like he is chastising them, as if they were misbehaving children.

We do not always realize that our emotions or mood-states directly influence whether or not we will stay *on the beam*. In other words, are you able to keep your emotions centered on, and your attention connected to, your spiritual nature? Or does your consciousness become frenetic, invariably pulling you off the beam and into the pit of despair, depression, anxiety or negativity? This is what was occurring with John. His negative emotions were getting the best of him and damaging his relationships with his clients.

These mood-states truly affect your behavior. When you are upset, bored or annoyed, are you trying to self-soothe by over-eating, drinking too much, gossiping, gambling, watching too much TV, staying overly busy or isolating yourself? These are some of the behaviors the ego-persona uses to pacify its reactions. They are forms of escape. They represent "getting out of Dodge" because the situation is causing discomfort, pain or annoyance. These behaviors keep us off the beam and further dilute our focus and attention on positive qualities.

If you approach your life problems from a surface, external perspective, and falsely believe that you should handle your problems in a vacuum of negative thought or feeling, you have just disconnected from and imprisoned your soul. This perspective is one of living by means of energy *going* *out* into the world in which the ego diminishes *you*.

Our ego, dominate-persona, is disconnected from the soul. It attempts to rationalize all our problems. It does so by causing us to keep our attention on issues that create anxious, critical, fearful, saddened, irritated, and clueless states. This usually muddies our perspective and only adds to our problems. We are now operating in the world of the detrimental Diminishing Aspects that do not bring uplifting or inner peace.

Alfie is a 43-year-old single career executive woman who came to me for coaching around self-esteem issues. One theme was taking place in many of her interactions: Alfie was basing her self-esteem on what others thought about her. She compared herself to her friends, neighbors, coworkers and enemies. She felt great when she was liked and lousy when disliked. She lived life on an ongoing, ever-ending rollercoaster of comparing herself to others.

Much of Alfie's inner dialogue and actual conversations with others were about feeling hurt, disappointment, anger and bitterness. She second-guessed her own decisions, and she felt that she was not smart enough, did not wear the right clothes, and seemed to be invisible in meetings at work. Her ego-persona was ruling both her outer affairs and her inner world and was creating a trail of discontentment, self-pity and self-blame; hence, her low self-esteem.

The ego-persona tends to react to situations as negative or positive, whereas a spiritual-centered response is patient and waits in a neutral state until the positive wins out. Generally, you can count on the ego reaction to be dramatic, sometimes even blowing problems out of proportion and making everything negative and bigger than it is. This was Alfie's tendency.

The ego-persona might also try to minimize the problem, thereby taking no action to resolve the situation. The ego, if possible, will try to avoid or deny the problem, or accuse others of being the problem. Both Alice, a teacher in a mid-western middle school who likes to shop, and her husband Tim, a truck driver who likes to gamble, have outstanding bills. They blame someone else for their inability to pay their debts on time. Thus, they choose the role of helpless victims rather than taking responsibility and taking steps to manage their financial situation.

The other side of the coin of the ego-persona is complacency, which opens the door to self-pity, in which the person feels, "there must be something wrong with me." The ego-persona has a farcical duplicity, either "I can handle this all by myself" (superiority complex) or "I don't have what it takes to handle this" (inferiority complex). Our ego-persona takes on many forms, feelings that are distracting you from forging a soul connection, cultivating growth, or reaching a deeper level to resolve your life problems.

This leads us to the next spiritual life skill: *Awareness that we are prone to distractions that keep us off balance and/or disconnected*. The *Distraction Factor* bars us from cultivating an inner calmness, poise, and centeredness. This keeps us from the environment of peace we need for refining our soul's Constructive Qualities.

Either we can view the problems and Diminishing Aspects in life as *obstacles* to living a fuller, more in-depth life, or we can see them as *sacred opportunities* we can use to learn about ourselves, thereby perfecting and applying an understanding of our true nature.

Problems provide a runway for learning about the triggers, reactions, and behaviors that keeps us off-center and push us into the quicksand of superficial living, *off the beam*. Obstacles or problems can become precious moments of discovering who we really are and what continued focus we need to maintain to transform them into blessings.

Take Mary, who struggled with a highly stressful job as a project management consultant to a multi-national retail chain. Due to her stress level affecting her health (i.e., weight gain, high blood pressure, ulcers), she sought out coaching to find effective ways to cope with the pressures of her job.

During her first coaching conversation, she identified experiencing multiple frustrations with her job, with certain employees and a dysfunctional project management team resulting in multiple communication, interpersonal conflicts and significant delays. The delays pushed back critical project-launch timelines. Mary was so invested in getting the project completed that she did not see her triggers and opportunities.

Through the process of engaging in several coaching sessions, Mary began examining her values, blind spots and life goals. By monitoring her self-talk and her emotional reactions to others, and by sorting through her career and life goals,

Mary started correcting the reactions, thoughts and behaviors that were draining her energy, damaging her health and well-being, and *keeping her off the beam*.

She began taking brief periods of time throughout her hectic day to reflect on how she wanted to be. She took two constructive qualities (Empowerment and Equanimity) to assist her with staying *on the beam*, feeling centered and productive.

Our soul needs to grow, advance, transcend, and transform former states of consciousness. Our ego-persona does not seek growth. It attempts to maintain the status quo. Our ego-persona puts us in a fancy prison, the penthouse suite, without even knowing that we are actually in prison. The prison is our constricted thinking, aggrandizement, amorality, and reactionary living. An almost magnetic pull rivets us to external living like filings to a magnet because it's very familiar, and it titillates our senses through fulfilling various desires and cravings. Nevertheless, it is false gold.

The *real* gold that we are looking for is within our self. As the old saying goes, "Your treasure is in your own backyard." Your soul is your gold. It is the genie in the lamp. It is a treasure that needs to be unearthed, refined, buffed-up and honed to sparkle like gold or crystal on a sunny day.

Remember Alfie, who came to me for life and professional coaching around self-esteem issues? After several sessions, she quickly began to identify how she had been setting herself up to live a lackluster, timid life. Through coaching exercises, she was able to identify her core values, strengths and unfilled needs. She was able to identify which events and people pulled her attention off the beam of her soul connection and ways to get back on the beam quickly. She used the constructive qualities of Authenticity, Empowerment and Equanimity to anchor her on her beam.

She found, through the course of coaching, a deeper measure of attunement, inner peace and satisfaction in her life, and she found that she connected to people in a more soul-centered, assertive and positive manner.

Ultimately, the questions that you must ask yourself are these:

What current experiences are testing me on how solid I am standing on my beam?

How am I learning to keep in touch with my soul's desires?

How do I know when my ego-persona is getting in the way?

What do I use as detours or distractions to distance myself from my soul?

What visualizations do I wish to have for my soul?

In what ways do I wish to talk to and pay attention in honoring my soul?

How do I know when it is my soul that is prompting me to act versus my ego-persona?"

Chapter 4

Committing to Your
Soul Advancement

Peace comes within. Do not seek it without.
~ Buddha

I f we don't know what to hold onto, we tend
to loosen our grip or get distracted or make
the decision not to fight because we don't
know what's important. This book is about making
choices concerning attention, attunement, and
aspiration for greater meaning and purpose. Each
person must make an ongoing commitment for
soul advancement. We must hold onto and fight
for the soul each second, minute, and hour of the
day.

This next spiritual life skill is *learning to take
still time to cultivate and advance our Twelve
Constructive Soul Qualities*. In doing this we help
our ego-persona become subservient to our soul.
We must find ways to reflect upon our soul and
connect with our soul's spiritual source, whether it
is God[1] or whatever you choose to call your soul's
spiritual source. What is important is the recognition that your soul is connected to a higher frequency of energy, which is your inner *geometry of*

divinity (GOD). There are geometric dimensions to GOD that extend beyond the human mind, feelings and willpower, that extend past time and space and transcend into the realms of Light, All Knowing, All Powerful and All Loving. GOD has solutions for every problem, condition or issue in our life.

You may be puzzled about the distinction between the soul and the soul's spiritual source, God. You may be thinking, *Are they not the same?* In many ways, they are, but there is one distinct difference: your soul is the individualization, your individual part, of the God-Source. The soul is a unique aspect of God in physical form or *manifestation*. The soul comes from God and will return to God.

Think of a tall, strong pine tree with many branches. The branches represent the different souls, and the roots and trunk represents the soul's spiritual source, God. Or think of a large fountain that springs forth thousands of streams of water. The base of the fountain is God and the multiple streams of water represent the souls. Or think of a drop of ocean water. The drop (soul) is distinct, but when it merges with the ocean (its source), it transforms into something larger, God.

These are all different ways of looking at how the soul is connected to something more than itself. If we are aware that we are greater than ourselves and that the source of our energy is from the One Supreme Source, then we will realize that we have an abundance of divine resources to call upon in handling life's challenges. However, if we believe that we are only the branch or the stream of water or the drop and are not part of that greater overall source, then we limit and restrict our potential for sustained joy, peace and happiness.

There are geometric dimensions to God, which are limitless and all-present that form the foundation of our existence. Those on a spiritual path are moving toward God through their soul, the substance of their life. For those who are uncertain or do not believe in God's existence, God is still continually trying to find ways to be a part of your life. You limit God's involvement by your disbelief, ego-persona and choices. If your attention only is focused on the superficial, than many distractions can end up taking you farther away from your beam. This disconnect, as if a lamp being unplugged from its electrical source, creates a void over time, a darkness, an emptiness in self and life.

When the ego-persona is always directed outward in an attempt to gain temporal pleasures and materialistic gain, the soul becomes subservient to the desires and surface living of the ego-persona. We then handle our life problems from a constricted and restrictive perspective, like the toss of the dice. Sometimes we get what we want and sometimes we do not. In either instance, we are living from the point of effect instead of

First Cause, which is God. The ego-persona lives from effect to effect to effect, where we are continually reacting, which results in our feeling overwhelmed and stressed.

Joe came to me for professional and life coaching due to feeling overwhelmed, as though his life was coming unglued. Over the years, his wife found him to be very critical, prideful and demanding. He viewed himself as a good husband because he had made the choice to forego some job opportunities that would have been more fulfilling but with less pay. He hated his current job, although it provided a good income. He was technically good at his job and was promoted to supervising others, which he found frustrating because they never wanted to follow his motto: "Just get the work done."

He found himself handling many employee conflicts and was frequently frustrated by the amount of time that took. When he was home, he was frequently in a bad mood with his family. His three kids—Mark, seven; Martha, six; and Marvin, three—wanted his attention and playtime with him. He also never would apologize for arguments he instigated with wife over the nine years of their marriage due to being tired and frustrated with his job. He thought jogging would help reduce his stress level, and it certainly did at times, but it also took away from family time, resulting in more conflicts with his wife. So he tried to stay at home more often and began surfing the internet instead, resulting in many hours spent in the den and even less time with his family. His wife began pulling away from him, becoming less engaged in family trips and conversations with Joe. She eventually asked for a separation.

Joe was shocked. He thought he was being a good provider, husband and father. Through the course of coaching and talking about behaviors that are on the beam and those that are off the beam, Joe began to see how he engaged in escapist behavior, negative self-talk and argumentative discussions with wife, kids and employees. He looked at the Twelve Constructive Qualities of the Soul and Diminishing Aspects of the Soul, and quickly identified attributes that had created his external living as he saw it now. He chose three qualities he wanted to focus on (kindness, gratitude/ appreciation and authenticity) to cultivate, within him and in his interactions with others, in the midst of his current situation.

Joe used his coaching sessions to explore, reflect and make some shifts in his attitude, feelings and behaviors toward his wife, children and employees. The process was painful for Joe because he had to look into the mirror and see his reflection in how he was toward himself and others in his life. He did not always like what he was seeing. But through the pain and challenges of confronting his negative behaviors (anger, criticism, worry, and anxiety, and other diminishing aspects), and honoring his constructive qualities, he was able to make progress.

The way to God is through attunement with your soul, a willingness to embark upon the journey of emptying yourself of inordinate desires (such as anger, jealousy, greed, resentment, bitterness, hurt), and the cultivation of the soul's desire for more of God in your temple. When this is consistently taking place, worldly gifts will naturally come to you, not from the ego-persona, but through alignment and obedience to God's laws.

You have probably had the experience of a friend calling you to share her day. She proceeds to complain, telling you how idiotic her boss is, and how annoying her husband can be. This negative engagement in speaking, thinking, feeling, and acting creates a destructive reality that is devoid of soul substance. It is the ego-persona (personality) at work wanting sympathy, attention and agreement that others are wrong and she is right. This right-and-wrong equation (e.g., someone must be wrong if I am right) holds us in a reactive mode. Hence, the soul's expression is muffled due to the reactive nature of the ego-persona.

For instance, if we pay attention to the conflicts in the world without examining how they relate to our internal reality, then we are doing ourselves a disservice. Are you familiar with the principle of Oneness, the interconnectedness of all beings? What we do to one person in the world we are, in actuality, doing to "ourselves". At a core level, we are all connected by vibrations, which can be described as the 'energetic web of life' or Oneness.

The next spiritual life skill or principle is, *All experiences teach us exactly what it takes to stay on the beam*. Instead of reacting negatively, we must learn how to keep our focus on the Twelve Constructive Soul Qualities. When we focus on such qualities as Empowerment, Kindness, Harmony and Authenticity, we are able to navigate gracefully through life.

However, problems in our lives may, at times, feel like they have their own magnetic pull, like the gravitational force of the planet. We are drawn to look externally for the solutions to our problems or to become upset about our problems without first going within to reflect and gain a better perspective on the situation.

Added to this external pull are the internal grumblings that manifest as worry, frustration, anxiety, doubt, and ingratitude, to mention a few. This boomerangs back to a negative mind-state where we are estranged from our soul, resulting in the belief that we have to resolve the problem completely through our ego-persona.

The ego is quick to be reactive instead of acting in alignment with what is in the best interest of the soul. In fact, there could be ongoing warring in our members[1], as Paul stated (Note:

Paul was an apostle of Jesus). The conflict is between the desires of the ego and the prompting and intuition of the soul. You know the difference between the two through vibration. Negative vibrations such as doubt, fear, hatred, criticism, and resentment, expressed through our words, thoughts, feelings and actions, create a worried and stressed consciousness that is not supportive to soul growth.

The soul is delicate, quiet and intuitive. If we do not trust these qualities in ourselves, we do not pay attention. If we do not give ourselves enough quiet time through self-reflection, meditation, yoga, tai chi, nature walks, or just slowing down to create sacred space and stillness, we cannot become connected. Soul cultivation is a process. It requires space. It requires patience. It requires, as fuel, the stoking of the Twelve Constructive Qualities. It ultimately requires giving attention to your inner promptings and having the audacity to make time for the blossoming of your soul.

Your ego is (or should be) submissive to the promptings and directions of your soul. The ego-persona should be taking directions from your soul. As previously stated, the ego-persona usually receives all our attention, is mostly reactive, and makes the decisions. The soul is where you begin to find deeper meaning, direction and purpose.

The Twelve Constructive Qualities that support and cultivate soul expansion and assist with staying centered (on the beam) are discussed in the next chapters along with the Diminishing Aspects.

Remember, this is a process, which is unique to each person. However, there are common themes that we can all entertain and with which we can all work. How you go about exploring and interpreting your life adventure will be unique to you and your soul. Always remember, the thoughts you think, the feelings you feel, and the actions you take will form the uniqueness of YOU. Enjoy your uniqueness and know that the spiritual path you are embarking upon provides an opportunity to transform your life from just superficial and surface living to core-value-based, spiritually inspired living. This will enable you to make your soul rightful heir of your castle and to utilize your ego-persona in only the highest ways that are dutiful to your soul.

Summary of Spiritual Life Skills and Principles:

1. Attention informs one's reality. Be aware of that to which you are giving your attention.

2. Be aware of the distractions that keep you off balance and/or disconnected. The *Distraction Factor* bars you from cultivating an inner calmness, poise, and centeredness.

3. Learn to take still time to nurture and advance the Constructive Soul Qualities and dissolve the damaging Diminishing Aspects. Find ways to reflect upon your soul and connect with your soul's spiritual source.

4. All experiences are teaching you exactly what it takes to stay *on the beam*.

PART II

Staying on the Beam

*A life without purpose is a languid,
drifting thing.
~ Thomas a Kempis*

Everything that limits us we must put aside.
~ *Jonathan Livingston Seagull*

We've been through the first four chapters of this book. The next three chapters revisit the Twelve Constructive Qualities that nourish the soul and discuss the Twelve Diminishing Aspects that create roadblocks to the soul's growth and advancement. I have categorized these qualities into Four Jewels that form a "cross of attunement and alignment." These are at the physical (behavioral), mental (thought), and emotional (feeling) planes, which become the pathways of the soul's journey to becoming more of an expression of God in manifestation.

Our thoughts, feelings and behaviors comprise who we are today. A host of variables, from family rearing to personal choices to life experiences, makes each one of us unique. The goal of this book is to provide the knowledge with which you may ponder and actively pursue what your soul needs to know, develop, and transform, by free will, in aligning with your Higher Source.

When you are able to tap into this deeper soul aspect of who you really are, you will find yourself on the path leading back to God. This life path is filled with self-discovery, cultivation of heart, inner contentment and the pleasure of deepening the connections to your soul and Higher Source. This path is not for the faint of heart. It is for the person who is willing to be tenacious, committed and focused to stay on the beam. When you do fall off, you will be willing quickly to jump back on.

The focus of the next three chapters will be on the unique facets of the soul's constellation. Remember, the answers we seek are within ourselves. I am providing some of the content and the questions to help you shift your gaze inward and toward your Higher Source, thereby experiencing an even more fulfilling life.

Summary:

The Twelve Constructive Qualities and Diminishing Aspects to the Soul

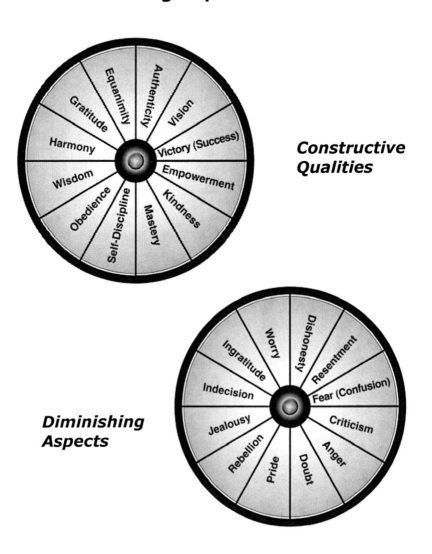

Constructive Qualities

Diminishing Aspects

Chapter 5

Four Jewels for the
Physical Liberation of the Soul

*You have the freedom to be
yourself, your true self, here
and now – and nothing can
stand in your way!*
~ Jonathan Livingston Seagull

The physical dimension of what the soul needs is analogous to building a house. You usually hire an architect to draw up the blueprints that provide the dimensions of the rooms and the style of house you would like to build. The construction foreman reads the floor plans (blueprints), cement is laid for the foundation, and the workers begin to build the rooms as specified by the blueprint design. Everything comes from the blueprint. Putting up sheet rock and installing the flooring, plumbing and electrical systems, etc. requires precision, resources and a systematic approach. In much the same way, the soul has specific requirements for building its divine foundation/home in life according with God's will. Each soul has a unique blueprint and foundation. The soul needs certain qualities to crystallize the blueprint into matter.

Harmony, Empowerment, Self-Discipline and Authenticity are the four sides of the soul's divine home (see the Soul's Physical Constructive Qualities and Diminishing Aspects chart). These are four types of structures: *Harmony* provides an "in-tune" atmosphere in which the soul can experience peace, centeredness and calmness, leading to growth. *Empowerment* strengthens the soul to stand up for truth and right (pure) motives in the midst of the ego-persona wanting to rule how to live life. *Self-Discipline* is the self-imposed standards, divine values, or rituals in which the soul willingly engages to walk a spiritual path in the world. *Authenticity* is the soul becoming more aware of who and what it is relative to its Highest Source.

The Soul's Physical Constructive Qualities and Diminishing Aspects Chart

This awareness becomes paramount for the soul in gathering enough momentum through the various experiences and soul qualities to secure and protect its divine birthright, and to evoke power over the ego-persona, who believes it rules your home or castle. All souls are born with a blueprint that holds the knowledge of our divine plan and purpose in life. This may be unclear or unknown, in part, due to our ongoing external, worldly focus of surface living.

I am reminded of the story about the chicken and the eagle. Eagle-Martha, at a young age, was raised on a farm with chickens and roosters. She behaved as a chicken, walked like a chicken, and even sounded like a chicken. She ate and played with the other chickens. Occasionally, Eagle-Martha had a glimpse that she might be different when she saw her reflection in puddles of water after rainstorms. She also felt an inner urge for doing something more and greater. One day another eagle, Eagle-Buddy, was flying high in the sky and saw Eagle-Martha below in the midst of the chickens on a farm. Eagle-Buddy swooped down and landed where Eagle-Martha was standing. He asked Eagle-Martha, "What are you doing amongst these chickens?" She said, "I'm not sure what you mean. This is my family." Eagle-Buddy said, "But you are an Eagle that flies and soars high in the sky! Here, come with me."

They walked to the top of a mountain. Eagle-Buddy showed Eagle-Martha how to take off, fly, glide and land. She skeptically said, "I can't do that!" Eagle-Buddy firmly said, "Yes, you can! And you will! Do not be limited by your chicken friends' teachings on how to just flutter your wings to be airborne for a few seconds! Your birthright is to spread your beautiful wings, take off, and soar, like all the eagles." Based upon what Eagle-Buddy demonstrated, she courageously took a deep breath and stepped off the mountain cliff. She excitedly screamed to Eagle-Buddy, "Look, look, I'm flying! Yes, I am able to see below with crystal clarity and soar like you soared!"

Our soul desires to soar! It knows what it wishes to do but has not been taught how to do it. It has existed in a pseudo-reality that caters to the ego-persona. Instead of soaring, the soul personifies the behavior of the chicken. The attributes of the chicken are confinement or imprisonment through *criticism, pride (arrogance), indecision, dishonesty* and other Diminishing Aspects of the ego-persona, which are discussed later. If more Diminishing Aspects are at work in your conscious and subconscious levels of your being, the ego-persona is certainly ruling your house.

Questions you can ask yourself are, "Do I find myself becoming irritable, angry or inharmonious with others or myself when things don't go my way? Am I sarcastic or critical toward people or events in my personal and professional relationships? Do I gossip about what another has or has not done? Do I think I am always right and have to let those around me know it?"

We have to be willing to reassess the structures we have built to perceive the world, and the manner in which we engage and react in the world. For example, Bob was satisfied with his job, but found his 18-year marriage stressful and unfulfilling. He and his wife frequently had verbal arguments around not having enough money to pay their bills. His wife felt that he did not show the initiative and drive to find a higher paying job. He secretly wanted more money and a more fulfilling job, but would never let "Mrs. Always Right," his wife, know that. He believed his wife had some good qualities but he could not stand her nagging. They had four well-behaved, precocious children. Bob described his wife as domineering, pessimistic and always pointing out his faults but never wanting to acknowledge her own faults. He found that their *criticism* in the marriage, the *arrogance (pride)* of his wife, his own *indecision* about looking for another job, and his *dishonesty* with himself had eroded both their marriage and his confidence in himself.

Bob was experiencing migraine headaches, restlessness, and difficulties getting a good night's sleep. He constantly worried about when the next fight would occur. He found himself (ego-persona) ruminating and nursing old hurts from past fights and planning what to say during their next verbal altercation. Without even knowing it, he and his wife were entrenched in the menageries of the ego-persona, the *Negative Aspects* that were draining vital energy from the marriage and his life.

From a soul perspective, Bob and his wife were acting like "chickens," not "eagles." Bob has to be willing to say, "Time out. How am I imprisoning my *own* soul, regardless of what my wife is saying or doing?" Fundamentally, we have to be willing to save and protect our soul from this type of caustic, negative energy (e.g., criticism, arrogance, indecision, dishonesty), whether it comes from within ourselves, or from the world outside ourselves (e.g., our partner).

Our soul is like a precious flame; when a strong wind comes along (i.e. hateful arguments), you must put a glass casing over the flame, like a hurricane lamp, for protection. Harmony, Empowerment, Self-Discipline and Authenticity are the Spiritual Qualities that enable the soul to feel protected and have the courage to do a graceful flip on the beam and land firmly. These qualities are what we need at the foundational level. We will be addressing some of the mental and emotional qualities in the upcoming chapters that the soul needs to experience integration and movement back to God. This creates purpose and meaning in life, which refines the virtues (the Twelve Constructive Qualities) that connect our soul's desire to unite with its Source.

Let us consider how to generate Empower-ment, Harmony, Self-Discipline and Authenticity within ourselves.

Space is provided after each of the four qualities to write down your reflections.

Empowerment is the soul experiencing the strength to soar in the world. The soul knows its Source, which created it for expression in the physical dimension. There is not a sense of separation but one of attunement with the concept that, "My Father and I (the soul) are one." By meditating upon this concept, we can step into a greater awareness of the immensity of God's presence in our life and invite God, our Father, to divinely strengthen us. This is not empowerment for the sake of "human power" to possess a person, object or thing. It is a sublime Divine power that strengthens the soul, enabling it to sense its greater purpose and a willingness to submit one's human will to the Will of the Father.

Questions to ponder:

How do I give my power away to another?

When do I feel spiritually empowered?

In what ways is this different from ego-persona power?

What would soul empowerment look like in my life?

Harmony occurs when there is inner peace and attunement. It enables the soul to experience the stillness of thought, words and emotions. The world is filled with noise, chatter, and chaos, but the stillness invites your Higher Source or God into yourself and enables you to observe how He dwells within you. You create the space for God's presence, and God gives you the experience of Himself. This requires regularly meditating on (or contemplating) the distinction between man-made harmony and God-Harmony. Invite God's Harmony into your silent moments and daily activities, and be open to the experience. It requires patience to listen beyond the stillness. It pushes you to release preconceived beliefs about self, man, and God or Higher Source.

Questions to ponder:

How do I create the inner space to listen to the promptings of my soul?

Has there been a time in my life when I felt an inner peace? What was that like?

Is that something I can re-create daily for myself? How?

How do I structure my day to have quiet moments or time?

Self-Discipline is the willingness to say no to certain ego-persona desires such as speaking harshly, acting badly, emoting harmful feelings, or thinking negative thoughts. Without self-discipline, there is no spiritual quest or path. Self-Discipline is achieved because you love God or Higher Source more than yourself, your desires, thoughts, and feelings. You love God with all of your heart, mind and soul. This becomes evident by where you place your attention (e.g., on the divine or human ego). Self-Discipline can manifest as the structure, guidelines, and restraints you follow to stay focused, and to not be distracted or derailed from your soul's desire for God. It is the process by which you surrender the lesser human desires that lure you to surface living only. It sometimes requires observing yourself and your habit-patterns, fasting, prayer, and/or setting aside time for contemplation to discern God's desire for your life. Habit-patterns are behaviors we engage in that can be automatic and constructive or destructive. Be alert for the destructive patterns and change them.

Questions to ponder:

How often do I monitor my thoughts and feelings?

How aware am I of my habit patterns? Are there any themes?

What would divine self-discipline look like in my daily life?

How is rigidity different from self-discipline?

Authenticity is the soul's realization of who and what it is. It is the realization that the more transparent your soul is, the greater the opportunity to be an instrument for your Higher Source or God. It is your soul's purest desire to become a unique representation of God in physical form. Authenticity is a genuine, conscious determination to be faithful to your soul. It requires fervent effort and communion. Authenticity merges with faithfulness to be "truthful" to self, just as all Twelve Constructive Qualities have the potential of merging with the soul, to unite with God, through the process of ascending daily by transforming the ego-persona energies and pseudo-desires of the world. This requires observation, curiosity, and creating space from fast-paced living to invite your soul and God to reveal more of itself to you.

Questions to ponder:

What would my soul consider to be my authentic self?

When am I being authentic vs. when am I deceiving myself?

What does being truthful mean to me in my life and relationships?

What does authenticity look like in my life?

The four jewels of Empowerment, Harmony, Self-Discipline, and Authenticity are the four pillars that form the structure for the soul to feel secure and safe. In the next chapter, we will discuss the four mental or *illumination jewel qualities* needed to liberate the soul.

Chapter 6

Four Jewels for the Mental Liberation of the Soul

Let nothing disturb thee,
Let nothing affright thee,
All things are passing.
God never changeth.
Patience gains all things.
Who has God wants nothing.
God alone suffices.
~ Saint Theresa of Avila

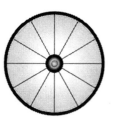

You are more than your human ideas and thoughts, but your thoughts pave the path to being on a "one-way street", a "two-way avenue", or a "super-highway" in how you live life. The one-way street is usually an expression of the ego-persona (energy *going out*). The two-way avenue is the expression of the soul (inner stillness plus outer activity). The super-highway is the expression of God flowing through the soul and the soul's striving to be more Christ-like[1] in thought, word and deed in order to be in the continuous figure-eight flow (see Chapter 1), which at higher frequencies merges into Oneness. What will be your choice?

As you are aware, our thoughts and emotions play a role in whether we choose a one-way street, an avenue, or a super-highway. In this chapter, we focus on the mental qualities that either become jewels through which the soul can radiate or rocks weighing down the soul, like a sack of stones sinking to the bottom of the ocean.

Underlying the Soul Qualities (Needs) for *Mastery, Wisdom, Equanimity, and Victory (Success)* is the precious yellow sapphire gem of Illumination. Illumination is the common thread that runs through these qualities. Throughout the lifetime, the soul is gaining—through daily, weekly, monthly, and yearly experiences—an illuminated, discerning perspective that triumphs over the mundane, narrow scrutiny of the human ego-persona. This consciously displaces the Diminishing Aspects of Doubt, Jealousy, Worry, and Resentment. Remember, one of the spiritual life skills is to learn through daily practice just how to make the ego-persona subservient to the soul. One step toward that end is for the soul to grow, in the Illumination flame-jewel qualities of Mastery, Wisdom, Equanimity and Victory (Success). This aids in weeding out ignorance from one's consciousness.

The Soul's Mental Constructive Qualities and Diminishing Aspects Chart

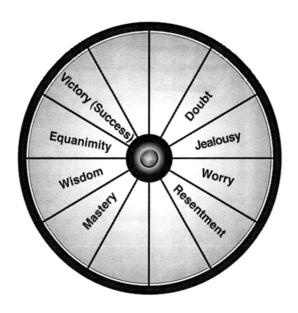

Do your thoughts jump around so much that you want to scream, "Stop it!" at yourself? Do you perseverate on situations that really get you upset? Do you feel like your thoughts are controlling you instead of the other way around? Many people find it difficult to let go of obsessive thoughts, thoughts that play in their head like a broken record. This usually occurs when we are reacting to something, be it a live event or our interpretation of the event. This revolving of our thoughts keeps us reacting and spinning on the periphery of self, surface living. The power of our thoughts, ideas and beliefs is amazing. We must gain mastery over them.

Our ideas and thoughts are like the electrical wiring in a house. We don't necessarily see all the wires that enable us to have electricity throughout the house, but we know it's there because we can turn on the lights. Our thoughts can influence the healthy functioning of our body or the dysfunction (i.e., dis-ease). Empirical research has shown the influence of negative thinking on the heart (e.g., cardiovascular disease).

Take a moment to reflect: Have you found it difficult to banish certain types of thoughts? Has an event taken place that evoked fear, worry, jealousy or some type of retaliatory thoughts, resulting in you mentally turning over the events in your mind to the point of finding it difficult to let go? This type of obsessive, repetitive thinking becomes a distraction for the soul, especially if the event is tied to any type of unresolved pain or hurt. It acts as static, interfering when you're trying to sense the promptings and direction of the soul.

Our mental reactions can be driven by intellectual pride coming from the ego-persona, along with a lack of discipline of the mind and the habitual negative patterns (thoughts) of the mind. The ego-persona has created the illusion through rationalization: "I have always thought, reacted and believed a particular way about certain situations/events in my life. Therefore, that's the way I am." What the ego-persona has *not* informed you of is that there are other divine ways of viewing, believing, perceiving, thinking and responding to life events. This is where the soul needs our support, which we can provide by mentally cultivating the jewels of Mastery, Wisdom, Equanimity, and Victory (Success).

The ego-persona likes to stay busy; however, these mental distractions fuel the ego to react and develop a momentum on entrenched reactionary patterns of Doubt, Jealousy, Worry, and Resentment at the conscious and subconscious levels. These reactionary patterns can become ingrained to the point where they become intense habit patterns that drain our soul energy and rule over us.

Have you experienced or met people who told you they felt suspicious, anxious or resentful most of the time? A man in his 40's told me that he was angry and resentful about his father leaving his mother, his three sisters and himself. He would get so angry that he would take it out on other people. He found that his resentment and anger had ruled him into his adult life. He had a nasty attitude and was quick to fight whenever he felt slighted by anyone. He knew that he was being destructive to himself and others by getting involved in fights and his excessive drinking, but he found it difficult to alter his thoughts and feelings about the past, so he engaged in retaliatory behavior.

These negative thoughts, feelings and actions make you believe, falsely, that you are doing something about your pent-up energy, but they're actually creating a sense of alienation from your soul. This moves you into looking farther outside of yourself to find answers and engaging in activities that only temporarily soothe your pain. This may also cause other problems, such as becoming addicted to drinking, gambling, overeating, shopping, having affairs, etc. We sometimes believe that if a person causes us pain then we have a right to cause them or others pain, even though the others might have had nothing to do with our original pain. The ego-persona is ego-centric and often focuses on retaliation and on nursing resentments.

These experiences create a density, a weighing down of consciousness that maneuvers the ego-persona into perceiving things from a limited, one-way perspective. It actually can encase the soul's desire from gaining spiritual illumination through developing a sense of Mastery, Equanimity, Wisdom and Victory in our lives. This is where our soul needs our help in keeping our attention, conviction, and intention on finding constructive ways to resolve our hurts of the past or present by cultivating one, or all, of the four jewel qualities. We can also utilize other professional resources, such as counseling or coaching, as needed.

Many of us will have some type of challenging situation(s) in our lives that pushes us off the beam, but falling off the beam is not the important part. What is important is how do we get back on? Getting back on the beam can be achieved by re-orienting your thinking about the painful situation, grieving the loss, and/or seeking professional assistance to support yourself in making specific changes in your beliefs, and gaining the wisdom and determination to transform yourself. It is the Jewels of Illumination, not the brittleness of intellectualism used by the ego-persona that provides the lighted path of knowledge to guide you through challenging situations.

The soul's thirst for illumination (spiritual understanding) has four qualities that balance the soul and enable it to move toward liberation from the ego-persona experiences and align with God. Let's explore these soul qualities.

Space is provided after each of the four qualities to write down your reflections.

Mastery is integrating the learning from life lessons, thereby providing the springboard for a deeper understanding of self. Were you ever curious about how Jesus gained the mastery in his life, allowing him to be recognized by God who said, "This is my beloved Son with whom I am well pleased!" There was a certain mastery Jesus gained in preparing for his mission of service. His mastery came through studying ancient and contemporary texts, spending time fasting and meditating, and attuning his consciousness to the Lord. In that way He was able to take dominion over the ego-persona. His soul became the rightful heir of His castle through the mental refinement of the qualities of Mastery, Wisdom, Equanimity and Victory (Success) (along with the other soul qualities) and then maintaining an "I am the GUARD" consciousness.

Questions to ponder:

How can self-mastery take place in my life?

What areas of my life, especially related to how I think, do I wish to master?

What knowledge and life experiences do I wish to integrate?

What needs to be re-configured or transformed in my consciousness (i.e., mental ideas, attitudes and beliefs) that will enable my soul to advance on the spiritual path?

Wisdom encompasses creative expression that integrates knowledge from our life experiences and soul "intuition" to provide service to others and the world. (This is different from Mastery, which focuses on the refinement of self.) It is giving away to others, as we deem appropriate through proper discernment, our knowledge coupled with real-life experiences. The ego-persona perverts this pure quality by jealousy and ignorance, becoming possessive and unwilling to share or coveting what someone has due to a sense of lack. Where there is wisdom there is no human lack. Wisdom is the instilling of a "God's mind" way of thinking: "What would Jesus, or any Saint, do in this situation?" I think of wisdom as "wise-dominion."

Questions to ponder:

What is the difference between wisdom and human intellectualism?

What does "Let that mind that was in Christ Jesus be within me" mean?

What does it look like in my life?

How would I know that I am enabling my soul to put on the mantle of wisdom in my daily affairs?

Equanimity is a centeredness that is poised and calm in the midst of any type of storm in life. It is nonattachment to the whirlwind of life, yet being very attached to the desire for God in your life. The more you are attached to the things in the world the less likely you will be attuned to your soul. Strong attachments can create worry, nervousness and anxiety when we think we won't get that promotion or pay raise, for example. Many times the outcome of not getting what we think we want is nervous tension, sadness or disappointment, which generates roadblocks for the soul's desire for God.

I am reminded of the story of Buddha (*Siddhartha*[2]). While meditating under a Bodhi tree, he was tempted by Mara. Then, several young women came to tempt and distract him from his meditation on God. He gently, with his right hand, did the *vaijra mudra* (earth touching gesture), which meant, "I shall not be moved." We sometimes need to have a mantra or word phrase going on in our mind to keep our attention on our spiritual goals. One such statement could be, "I shall not be moved."

Questions to ponder:

What is really important to me in my life? Why are these things so important to me?

Are these things for the glory of the ego-persona or for my soul advancement and God?

What does equanimity look like in my daily affairs and life?

How can I be unattached to things and continue to love all life?

Victory (Success) knows no defeat because victory has the knowledge of what the situation requires. It is a spiritual awareness that your soul is centered in God and passing the initiations that comes along in life. Regardless of what occurs in the world, you are anchored in God's victory for your life. What is success for one person might look different for another. Think of the saints who had great afflictions in their bodies. They might have appeared unproductive to the world, but for the Lord each one performed a mighty service. These souls remained constant and true to maintaining an inner Christ standard. The ego-persona seeks outer accomplishment, which is transitory. When the ego-persona does not achieve its desired goal, it becomes resentful, revengeful, or retaliatory. Victory is a state of consciousness that transcends human concepts and is focused on the soul achieving its victory, ascending daily back to God. It is not the victory of the human but the victory of the soul.

Questions to ponder:

What does Success or Victory look like to me?

What does Divine Victory or Success look like for my soul in my daily dealings?

What is the mental shift in attitude, belief or perception needed?

How has the knowledge that I have gained throughout my life experiences assisted me in achieving a sense of victory or success?

Changing ideas, beliefs, and thought patterns can occur in the blink of an eye, but for many of us it is a process of discernment, attunement, and persistence. These four jewel qualities support us in molding our thoughts to reflect more the desires of our soul and the desires of God. By contemplating or reflecting on the phrase *Divine Mind of God* we open the portal for God's illumination to flow into us, which allows us to make wiser decisions in all our affairs.

We have discussed the Qualities/Needs for the physical and mental dimensions that cultivate and nourish the soul to aspire toward God. We shall now turn our attention to the emotional jewels that liberate the soul to continue to adore and worship God.

Chapter 7

Four Jewels for the Emotional Liberation of the Soul

Be Kind!
Remember everyone
you meet is fighting
a hard battle.
~ T. H. Thompson

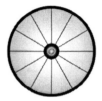

God plays a hide and seek game with each of us. He is curious to see how well we refine our soul through the choices we make. Are our choices in attunement with His will or our human will (i.e., ego-persona)? There are multiple desires at the physical, mental, and emotional levels, and the choices we make brings us closer to God or sets us on a course traveling away from God. Just as much as we want to be loved by God, God desires for us to lovingly adore Him, similar to the figure eight flow. This moves us from the one-way street of existence to the super-highway, based upon the commitment of our daily activities to the Glory of God or Higher Source, through the jewels of *Kindness, Obedience, Gratitude and Vision.*

You may not always realize it, but if you look back on your day, week, or month, you may quickly see that God has not been invited into your conversations, into the tasks you performed, into your work projects, into the discipline of your child, or into your relationships. You may think of yourself as emotionally separate from God. You must embrace God as being where you are.

As you release more of the ego-persona ways, as well as *Anger, Rebellion (Disobedience), Ingratitude and Fear (Confusion)*, you will find a shift occurring within (see The Soul's Emotional Constructive Qualities and Diminishing Aspects Chart). How would you now deal with situations from the past, where you once felt alone or anxious? Now you find an inner strength, a conviction and a devotion to that "spirit spark" (soul) within you. Now your soul is graced with the unfolding of God's presence in the totality of who you are... an individualization of God or Higher Source.

The Soul's Emotional Constructive Qualities and Diminishing Aspects Chart

The ego-persona's drive for wealth, fame, and material goods divides our attention on, and our vision of, God. Our vision and attention become scattered on all of the "things" we want, devoid of God being the Source for all of our needs. Since we have not entertained the notion of how to live our life by a Christ- or God-like standard, we live by the ways of the world.

If someone is not kind toward me, then I will *hate* or dislike them. If someone jumps the turnstile to catch a train in the subway station, that gives me permission to do the same (*disobedience* to the laws of the land). If people do not say "thank you" to me, I certainly will not give them the time of day by saying "thank you" to them (*ingratitude/insensitivity*). If someone does not tell me the truth, that gives me the license to lie and make up a story when I need to (confusion/*deception*).

It is through the arrogance and pride of the ego-persona that we are enslaved to the mundane ways of the world. Whether we know it or not, we have just created major roadblocks in consciousness. Our soul becomes weighted down and caked over by the densities of our choices in the world. We can spiral into questioning the meaning of life and may even become bitter, sarcastic, and angry because of the hollowness in our daily affairs. As the 14-year-old teen mentioned in an earlier chapter, "If there is no meaning to life, then I would rather not exist." This sense of separation occurs through totally living in the outer world and not being anchored in a soul-awareness of God's existence.

The development, refinement, or cultivation of the qualities of Kindness, Obedience, Gratitude and Vision transforms you into being an instrument of His grace, rather than the aggrandizement of the ego-persona. What God is searching for is our awareness of His "pure desire" that manifests as right desire and choice. The desire of the soul is to become God's instrument in the earth. The adoration and *Obedience* to God's laws stokes the fires of *Divine Love* and single-eyed *Vision* (instead of dual eyes for the effects in the world) to seek God first, by which all else is given to the soul in daily living.

There is a peculiar dynamic, which occurs with the ego-persona. The ego-persona is quick to seek transitory, sensual pleasures and uses God's energy that allows you to live and move, to fulfill surface pleasures. Since we have free will, God waits to see if we will choose Him or the desires of the ego-persona.

This choice can come in the form of where we place our *Attention,* one of the Spiritual Life Skills mentioned earlier. It could come in the form of being so focused on the distractions of the world (i.e., dealing with our problems) that we lose sight of God, (i.e., another Spiritual Life Principle). Or by electing to stay busy with our jobs, relationships, or recreational pursuits, we never quite make time for reflection and stillness (another Spiritual Life Principle). We can also be so engrossed in the problems of living that we do not even consider how we can help those less fortunate than ourselves. For the ego-persona it is always "about me" or "what can I get" or "what you owe me" or "what's in it for me." It is about the dispersing of energy (*energy going out*) and not the conserving of your life energy to be the "light bulb" for God.

Life provides us a precious sacred opportunity to choose to magnify God's qualities in our life, including those soul qualities already mentioned in Chapters 4 and 5 as well the qualities discussed in this chapter: Kindness, Obedience, Gratitude and Vision. Hopefully, we will actively wrestle with and win over or dissolve the four negative attributes of Anger, Rebellion (Disobedience), Ingratitude and Fear (Confusion), which manifest due to ignorance (e.g., ignoring the laws of God, such as the "golden rule").

These spiritual qualities—Kindness, Obedience, Gratitude and Vision—nourish the soul like a mother providing nourishment to her baby. They provide nurturing energy in our interactions and relationships with our partner, children, colleagues and strangers. One of my clients was given the assignment of being kind at work and at home. He was a little skeptical but he began to do what he thought would be kind. He actually told me that he looked up kindness to get a better idea about what he needed to do to show kindness in his interactions. Once he had that awareness under his belt, he practiced kindness at home with his wife. He reported back that he had actively listened more instead of cutting off his wife from talking, was more understanding instead of trying to fix the problem with wife, he spoke in calmer intonations, shared more of his thoughts with wife instead of keeping them to himself, smiled more and was warmer in his interactions. He stated that he was astonished how by working on this one constructive quality he quickly changed a long-standing problem of his wife feeling less under-stood and devalued by him. He liked engaging in this constructive quality. He felt more relaxed and open, instead of tight and constricted.

These four qualities—Kindness, Obedience, Gratitude and Vision—have the underlying themes of a ruby jewel, radiating the divine energies of surrender, sacrifice, selflessness, and service. These emanate from the heart, leading to a profound dedication to the Heart of God. God is holy and pure and, in turn, through devotion your soul becomes holy and pure.

You must be vigilant about what you allow to occupy your mind, your space, and your feeling world. You must be mindful of your daily conversations and deeds. A standard of divine protection surrounds your soul when you make the commitment to stay on the beam. By being keenly aware that you do not wish to do anything that would be displeasing or offensive to God, you do not allow into your consciousness any lower vibrations of the ego-persona, such as Anger, Disobedience, Ingratitude and Fear (Confusion).

A wonderful illustration of this type of relationship between the soul's pure desiring and commitment for God and God's ministration to the soul is in *The Practice of the Presence of God* by

Brother Lawrence. Even though Brother Lawrence never lived in the 21st Century, where we have to be concerned about the ongoing challenges of money, job transitions and a wife or children who can take us "off the beam," he provides a glimpse and some pointers on how to focus toward God.

This story transcends theological doctrine and training. Brother Lawrence was a monk who worked as a cook in the kitchen of a monastery. He lived a simple life of devotion, practicing *loving kindness, obedience, gratitude* and the holding of a clear *vision* in his affairs. He dedicated all of his conversations, daily work, and activities to the glory of God. In other words, whatever he did throughout the day, he dedicated to God. He saw himself as the instrument of God. He allowed Spirit to flow through him like crystal clear water flowing down a mountain.

He shares a story in his book about traveling to another country to conduct business. He told the Lord that he did not know how to do the task (buying certain goods) his superiors had requested. He felt he did not have the education, experience, or business acumen to be successful in completing his assignment. He prayed daily to God and asked that the Lord use him, heart, head and hand. He retreated to the inner-chamber of his heart, knelt and prayed with a humble heart in child-like wonder. He adored, loved, and praised God for all of his daily blessings. He loved God tirelessly for His "infinite goodness and perfection" in his life. He would say to the Lord, "O, my God, since Thou art with me, and I must now, in obedience to Thy commands, apply my mind to these outward things, I beseech Thee to grant me the grace to continue in Thy presence; and to this end do Thou prosper me with Thy assistance, receive all my works, and possess all my affection."[1]

Obedience was one of the cornerstones, along with *love* of God, *gratitude* for God's presence, and *vision* of seeing himself as an instrument of God's will, that enabled Brother Lawrence to be successful. He found that all of his business dealings went smoothly. He met the right people at the right time, had the right conversations, and was able to successfully complete his business in the world. He was amazed! He gave *all* glory to God and saw himself as God's handiwork. As Saint Theresa of Sienna said, "Thou thee all, I the nothing."[2]

Brother Lawrence demonstrated in a profound way that he truly loved God with all his heart, mind, and soul. God was the receiver of all of His feelings, promptings, thoughts, deeds, and works. He learned the beauty of filling his mind and being with the infinite power, love and wisdom of Almighty God. He spent all of his intervals, throughout his days, in heart-felt prayer and communion.

Brother Lawrence epitomizes the qualities of Kindness, Obedience, Gratitude, and Vision, which expand the heart to unite with the Heart of God. The pulsing of your heart is truly the pulsing of God's heart because you become one. Jesus said, "When you see me, you see the Father." You move from existing in the world of the ego-persona to existing in the consciousness of God. This requires a discerning, surrendering, and refining process. You must be willing to give up old patterns of existence of the ego-persona to have the greater presence of God in your life. It is God who allows you to transcend the transitory world of effect by refining your "cross of attunement and alignment" of Kindness, Obedience, Gratitude, and clear Vision.

How do we consciously cultivate the soul's nurturing qualities of Kindness, Obedience, Gratitude, and Vision? Below are some thoughts and questions to ponder.

Space is provided after each of the four qualities to write down your reflections.

Kindness (a feature of love) is selfless and unconditional. Human love is fickle and can change as the weather changes. God's love is what we are striving to express in our daily lives through kindness. Kindness shows compassion, care, and concern for oneself and others. It is felt *within* the heart and is sent *from* the heart. Divine love uplifts our soul to feel as though we are a part of something greater than our self. Divine love is discriminating and acts based upon wisdom and the strength of conviction. Love is the "light of victory everlasting." The soul is able to transcend the human fragilities of the ego-persona perspective, by purifying motives, cultivating an intense desire for God, and holding a clear Vision in the midst of living in the world of effects.

Questions to Ponder:

How am I unkind or insensitive in my words and actions toward self and others?

What does it mean for me to be kind in thought, word and deed?

If I were to increase kindness toward myself and through my service to others, what would that look like?

How does worthiness and kindness relate to how I live my life?

Obedience is essential to garner a greater measure of God's presence in your life. Obedience is the willingness to sacrifice your human desires and to attune genuinely to your soul's promptings. It means taking the time to discern the difference between the soul and your ego-persona's desires. You need to be patient with your soul and know that confusion may arise due to the strong pulls of the ego-persona, which can manifest as overt or subtle forms of rebellion and disobedience. You must be alert to the ways in which you sabotage yourself by being mentally, emotionally, physically, or spiritually rebellious.

God has released universal laws through the various prophets and saints. Because of our devotion to God, we willingly obey His principles or commandments. We ponder how they are applicable for living in the 21st century. We consider obedience and self-discipline. *Obedience* is an intense devotion to God's presence in one's life and the willingness to uphold His precepts. *Self-Discipline* is the self-control one willingly applies to one's personal desires and actions.

Take Lisa, who wants to stop flying into road rage when cut off while driving, which requires a certain degree of self-discipline. Through a strong faith and love for God to no longer engage in what she considers a "bad habit," she systematically takes the steps to break the habit pattern. She enlists professional help and family support to change the habit because she wants a closer relationship with God or Higher Source. There are certain personal human habits of the ego-persona, which create barriers to achieving a closer relationship with God. Road rage (anger) fits into this category. The soul desires to be like a windowpane for God's rainbow rays to shine through. To be this refractory prism of Light, obedience to God's precepts becomes paramount.

Questions to Ponder:

What needs to change in my life to walk the path of obedience to my soul and God?

What would this look like at work and in my daily life?

How do I define what it means to be obedient to my soul?

Are there ways that I rebel against the promptings of my soul?

Gratitude is the expression of thankfulness for God's love in your life and in those around you. It is being pleased and thankful for all that your soul receives. Gratitude builds or fortifies the bridge and accelerates the crossing through attunement, to God. Appreciation, admiration, and the holding of God in high esteem creates an energetic frequency, or vibration, that God receives and sends back to us in the form of inspiration, talents, and spiritual advancements along the path. It is the spiritual glue, along with love and the other qualities, that binds the soul to God. Gratitude helps dissolve insensitivity and hardness of the heart. It evokes sensitivity to God's presence and provides direction in our lives.

Questions to ponder:

What does gratitude mean to me?

How do I express gratitude to God, my family, and others?

In what ways am I insensitive to the needs of others and myself?

How am I gracious even when others are rude and condescending toward me?

Vision is about seeing past the human form to the essence, rather than deceiving or confusing ourselves by paying so much attention to the world of effects. It is moving from dual-eye vision to single-eye vision. In other words, it is moving from seeing things through our human eyes, to holding the highest vision for ourselves and others, even in the midst of negativity. It is training one's self to see past the world of effects to seeing "First Cause" (God) in the midst of our daily trials. It is holding the highest vision at the soul and/or blueprint level for people in our lives. The soul is the individualization of God in matter. It is the soul that we see as being perfect in God. This does not mean we are not aware (and act accordingly) of a person's ego-persona, fears, weaknesses, or problems, but we realize that God has a solution. As we take quiet time for contemplation and attunement through the cultivation of the Twelve Qualities of the soul, we become inspired with meaningful reflections and answers.

How often do we ask ourselves, "What is the truth in this situation?" If we do not ask the question, we don't receive the answer. There is an old adage that the "call compels the answer." We need to be more inquisitive and receptive to wanting to know the answer. I have had people tell me that they are afraid (fearful) of asking the question because they are not sure they really want to hear the answer. This closes the door to our connection to God and moves into a horizontal relationship with human ego-persona of others.

We can make decisions based upon the human sympathies of the ego-persona and not on the Christic (or Christ-like) Truth of a situation. We have to be open to changing our responses and behaviors because the ego-persona will frequently try to deceive, deny or detour us from the Truth. The soul's substance comes from our willingness to uphold what is true, noble and pure in the person or situation, and to rebuke the lie, the half-truths and the detours of the ego-persona.

Life is about evolving and not becoming so comfortable in our creature comforts that we lose sight of why we are here—to see the best in others and to gain the experience to become co-creators of our lives with God.

Questions to Ponder:

How do I know that I am being truthful (honest) with myself?

When do I deceive myself about people or situations?

How can I try to see family, friends, and co-workers in the highest Vision and be compassionately truthful?

What types of situations, relationships, or people pull me off the beam of being truthful?

Underneath these soul qualities of Love, Obedience, Gratitude and Vision, is the ruby rose quartz (jewel) of devotion and worship. This gem is the devotion to something higher than one's self and a willingness to elevate one's thoughts, feelings, and service in honor of one's love for God. This is not the human love that is usually possessive, but the Lord's qualities of Love, which are universal and eternal.

The ultimate goal is to provide the soul with the qualities that create a yearning to strive for and transform the lesser elements within us and to instill a sense of the sanctity and balance in your feelings and emotions, which liberates the soul. The ego-persona is less concerned about sanctity and more concerned about appearances; when the ego-persona is subservient to the soul, your consciousness shifts to an expanded awareness of the simplicity and intricacies of God. Our uniqueness perceives the presence of God in our daily affairs.

Chapter 8

Living a Daily
Soul-Filled Life

*A gem cannot be polished without friction, nor a
man perfected without trials.*
~ Chinese Proverb

Navigating on a super highway or staying "on the beam" are analogies for understanding the spiritual life principles and skills needed for the striving soul to evolve and be liberated. The art of staying "on the beam" takes an awareness of form (physical jewels), the precision of movements (mental jewels), and the artistic grace and flexibility (emotional jewels) of the routine all of which increase the likelihood of staying "on the beam." Blending all these factors results in a lively and inspiring performance! Life is asking our soul, given the right resources and focus, to carry out a masterful performance every day of our lives.

The Twelve Constructive Qualities (jewels) surrounding the soul refines the soul's evolvement and expansion, just as the Twelve Diminishing Aspects become messengers that quickly takes us "off the beam" of living a soul-spirit-filled, purposeful life. The core function of the Twelve

Constructive Qualities is to enlighten and support the soul in glorifying God in ourselves and in all of our affairs. You can also think of these Twelve Qualities as a magnificent mosaic in which each piece plays a valuable role in forming the beauty of the picture, affording the soul the "sacred opportunity" of living a spiritual life through our daily affairs.

Many factors blend into the uniqueness of who we are. We must consider what experiences are being brought into our lives as tests of our concentration, commitment, and courage to stay focused on our spiritual path while handling our daily commitments. I believe that the single quality that gives us the tenacity and dogged determination to stay connected to God is Divine Love. It is the oscillating of the Twelve Qualities on the wheel that intensifies into the Supreme Love of God. God's love is a powerful vibration that ripples across the universe. It creates lightness in our being and an inner calmness in our interactions with others. I have never known a person who has experienced God's Love to simultaneously feel down trodden, mean spirited, or alienated from self or others.

Love is the magnet that draws God closer. Just as much as God loves us, He will also test us to see just what our capacity is to Love each day. Love is the glue that binds our inner self to the Greater self, God, and His love, wisdom and power. Love is the means by which we are willing to let go of our human will and our desires (ego-persona) for the ultimate divine Will and Direction. The more we cultivate love in daily interactions, service, and ourselves, the more God fills in the spaces of our being with His magnificent vibration of Love. This Love has the capacity to dissolve past hurts, pains, and negative experiences. The more we forgive, the more we free up our self to Love, knowing that we surrender our worldly experiences to God, including hurt and pain

We live with free will and have the choice to either embrace the ego-persona or the "soul's path" to God. The soul is learning to be more Christ-like in the demonstration and cultivation of Love. It is not a matter of *whether* there will be a wrestling within between opposing forces, it just a matter of *when* and *for how long.* When this wrestling occurs, think, *How can I relinquish the ego-persona struggle for dominance and make a conscious, intentional decision to uplift the divinity within me?* This type of questioning acknowledges "God within" (the soul) as being far greater in importance than the pseudo-desires of one's ego-persona. This does not mean that you will not experience discomfort, but it does mean that you are willing to move through the discomfort, letting go of old baggage (of thinking, feeling and behaving) for the Love of God's principles, virtues, and presence in your life.

In order for Love to expand within us, we need to think, feel, and behave as if God is at our side.

We must know that God is within us. We have to be willing to engage in conversations or chats with God, Our Father. We have to build our trust in knowing that God is walking with us through all the circumstances in our life. It is through trust that we build faith, believing in those things that are not visible through the dual eyed vision.

There are many dimensions to God (*geometry of divinity*), which enable Him to work in marvelous ways in our life based upon our receptivity and our capacity to Love. We have to get out of the way of our smallness (ego-persona) to begin to see or sense God's "bigness" in our lives. In sensing God's immensity through prayer, meditation, and reflection, we begin to understand that God is truly with us, through the "Law of Oneness." This strengthens and anchors us in the Presence of the Lord. This, thereby, allows us to be more of God where we are. Is that not awe inspiring?

The ego-persona has its place in our life. It ties into the unique talents, expressions, and contributions of the soul in the world. Through right choices, we consciously transmute or transform these negative aspects, which are like barbed wire around the soul, into filigree wires of light to support the soul's mission. As the human ego-persona is placed under the dominion of our soul through mastering certain life experiences, we become Christ-like in our inner and outer expression. Because of our willingness to uphold a higher standard through incorporating some or all of the Twelve Qualities, and to having dedicated our self to living a God-centered life, we become the embodied representative of God's Love, Wisdom, and Power.

Implementing a plan, a strategy, and a means to actively monitor ourselves is critical to soul evolution. This is the same as implementing a plan to achieve any worthwhile goal, and the monitoring is similar to the hall monitors in school who made sure that you were going where you said you were going. The most important areas to monitor are our thoughts, emotions (reactions), and behaviors. We need repeatedly to ask ourselves, *How am I staying connected to God today? How am I submitting my ego-persona desires to the direction of my soul, which is an outpost of my God-divinity?*

Only through humility are we able to see the flaws within our "diamond of self" from the smallest to the largest blemish. We can readily see the larger flaws and we can go about rooting them out. The smaller inclusions require us to be vigilant and open to hearing others' feedback, along with self-reflection and willingness to change. The key ingredient is *humility*. It prevents us from becoming offended, defensive, or retaliatory in our thoughts, words or deeds. In our humility, we do not become reactionary; rather, we are able to see others as messengers sent to help us be aware of our blind spots. This requires a willingness to let go of emotional reactivity, human pride, arrogance, and the other aspects of the ego-persona. It is submitting all that you value in this world to God first, to the fires of Love, Wisdom, and to His will and direction.

Here are a few simple, daily spiritual approaches in achieving soul liberation and evolution:

1. Choose one or two of the Twelve Qualities (see below). Focus on cultivating them in all that you think, say, and do in life. Read about, think of, and feel deeply that virtue in your life from the time you wake up in the morning until you tuck yourself into bed at night. Do this until the virtue is second nature to you. Did you know that our human body sheds 1% of its cells each day? Just think about that: in 100 days you can have a new body. Similarly, in 100 days you can have a nice momentum toward God. Use a calendar to mark through each day toward your goal.

Constructive Qualities to the Soul

2. Be observant of your thinking patterns, emotional reactions, and situations that trigger counter-productive thinking and "emotional dramas" (charged melodramatic reactions). These thinking ruts or emotional dramas usually show up in our lives due to misperceptions, unresolved past memories, disappointments in life events, or negative interactions with others. When you find your thoughts and emotions "revolving," like a reel of film, in negativity, it is time to challenge these

energies. This may be in the form of affirming the Truth about who you really are (i.e., God in manifestation); or being quiet and meditating; or using breathing exercises, such as diaphragmatic breathing, to center yourself. You may become involved with a coach or counselor to support your efforts to consciously change certain habit patterns so you think differently and feel different.

3. Learn to take command and control over the energies causing restlessness, distractions, and scattered activities in daily living and in your body. If you want stillness in your energy, then *be* still. Take time to sit for three to four times per day for roughly five to ten minutes to still the self. You must face a situation, a distracting thought, or an annoying feeling, and then you must rise above it. You are more than your thoughts, feelings, and events. The ego-persona sees things from a restricted view. God within you sees things from an unlimited, eternal view.

4. Look at your consciousness as a garden where you have the opportunity to grow beautiful flowers such as roses, tulips, and azaleas, or where you can grow weeds. Gratitude and kindness are like the fertilizer and "de-weeder" in your garden. It is through the cultivation of the spiritual garden of gratitude and kindness, your soul is nurtured, bathed in light, and grows. Find ways that you can be grateful and/or kind nine

times or more per day, every day, concerning the events in your life from your past, present, and future.

5. Forgiveness is a powerful healer of many of life's situations. It is in the "for giving" of others that we liberate our cells (body and consciousness) from the weight of unhappiness, discontentment, ill will, resentment, and the Twelve Diminishing Aspects. Forgiveness is a form of mercy that God gives to us for our errors, which in turn we can give to others who may have wronged us. In forgiving, our energy is released, our load is lightened, and we are given more freedom to Love God and others. We must continue to ask Him for His lovely virtues to occupy our very being. Learn to forgive your evolving self and be compassionate toward the people in your life.

6. Be very careful of that on which you focus your attention. Do not become fixated on the things that you do *not* want. Many times when we are emotionally upset, we have, revolving in our minds, the negative event(s) that only add fuel to the fire of our discontentment. Resolve the problem in a timely manner by asking for God's Light into the situation and focus your attention on what you know is true, uplifting, and divine in the situation.

7. Every day reach up to the Heart of God. Visualize it as a huge sun above you. Envision that you are giving your God Presence a big hug. Symbolically, you are giving daily recognition for God's presence and service in your life. Ask your soul each day, "What is the highest service that I can give this day?" Listen and be obedient to your inner promptings throughout the day. You will meet people or be involved in situations that will afford you the opportunity to give an aspect of your/God's Love, Wisdom, and Strength. It is through this process of giving to others through your God Presence that you magnetize a greater portion of God's Spirit each day.

8. Remain conscious of the fact that whatever you do and receive is by the grace of God and not your ego-persona. You would not be able to move your arms and legs if it were not by the grace of God's energy flowing through you. It is only by God's gracious presence and by the power of God within you that you are able to experience another day. We need frequently to remind ourselves that we are using God's energy every moment of the day. "This is God's intelligence, love, and/or strength that allows me to _____."

9. Any of the Twelve Diminishing Aspects can takes us "off the beam" into the depths of feeling unworthy. Which ones can you identify (see Diminishing Aspects of the Soul)? Remember, the

God within you (your soul) *is* worthy. The human will always be prone to error. Just as Gandhi did in his life, be willing to learn from your mistakes, make corrections through self-discipline, and be a disciple of truth and compassion. Through these practices, one evolves to higher states of consciousness, which in turn leads one to God. God in you is worthy of being joyous, happy, and content. Train your consciousness to remain centered on God's Love for you, for your energy flows where your attention goes. If you focus on condemning others, you are actually forming a matrix of condemnation of self.

Diminishing Aspects to the Soul

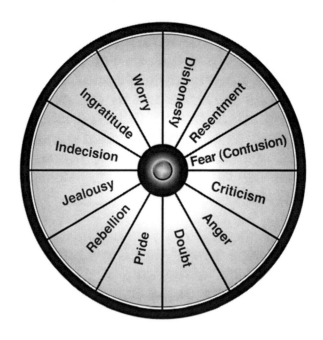

10. Practice love and inner calmness every day and be vigilant that your thoughts, words, and deeds do not engage in activities that are contrary to Love. With focus on increasing the positive oscillation of your wheel, through the monitoring of your thoughts, feelings, and actions, you magnify Love. The more you magnify the Twelve Constructive Qualities of Love, the greater the acceleration in the spinning. Higher vibrations or frequencies of Light-Love magnetize you to the hub of the wheel where God resides.

11. Find a way to quiet the inner and outer self so you can hear, sense, and feel the presence of God. Meditation has been used by the great sages and Tibetan masters to contact the great Source of Being, God. Meditation increases introspection and the "crystal cord of light," which provides contact, expansion, and strengthening through daily meditation. Find a meditative practice that works with your lifestyle and perform it regularly.

12. Find ways to challenge yourself to be an exceptional person each day. It is in striving for the excellence of God's Goodness in your life that you are willing to let go of the old thoughts, feelings, and behaviors and allow for the gifts of God to flow in you. Are there ways that you can hold yourself accountable to your specific, spiritual goals each day?

Remember, the ultimate goal for the soul is the ability to reflect God's glory to the outer world. The focus of life is to learn from our past, take stock of our present, and strive toward God. Your striving soul is a unique piece of the whole of God. Our souls are eagles hoping to be the messengers of God's love, truth, and service. It is by our *daily choices* that we elect to free our soul and acknowledge the power of God within to direct our daily affairs.

Our human habits, familial, and/or social conditioning will constantly try to pull us back to allowing our ego-persona to be in the driver's seat of our affairs. It will seem like this human pattern is very natural. To the contrary, it is unnatural to the striving soul. It is why over time people feel unfulfilled in life and search for something more and/or deeper. Your soul wants more from life. We do not always know where to turn to satisfy this hunger. It is as though you are in search of something but just do not quite know what. This is the same as wanting something different to eat but not being sure what it will be until you have eaten several things. Then you bite into something and you have a sigh of relief: "Yes, that satisfies my hunger!"

I wrote this book to satisfy a deep, abiding hunger of the soul for expression and connection to one's God source. I have consistently said that *we usually live life through our ego-persona and based upon what we see in society*. We strive so hard to obtain praise, acceptance, and personal recognition from family, friends, and work associates. We base our values and achievements on what others have accomplished. We think that this is what life is about.

It is my hope that through reading this book, you have set your feet upon the spiritual path of leading a more fulfilling and service-filled and sacred existence. You now know what it takes for your soul to stay "on the beam" and for you to "soar" like the eagle!

Notes

Chapter 1
Outer Versus Inner Realities: The Twelve Qualities of the Soul

1. Christ-like is a term representing a *universal, spiritual standard,* a state of consciousness. The term represents a constellation of divine qualities, virtues, characteristics or attributes that form the consciousness; a way of being and living irrespective of person. Jesus, Buddha, Krishna, Yogananda, Zoroaster, St. Catherine. St. Francis and all the great sages and saints throughout history came into embodiment, demonstrated, and validated a higher divine standard, consciousness and way of living in the world leading back to One's Source.

2. Vanzant, Iyanla, *One Day My Soul Just Opened Up*, (New York: Simon and Schuster (Fireside), 1999, preface.

Chapter 4
Committing to Your Soul Advancement

1. God is the term used throughout this book. The reader is invited to replace this term with a word or phrase that honors his/her

relationship with a Higher Infinite Source or Presence.

2. Romans 7:23/KJV

Chapter 6
Four Jewels for the Mental Liberation of the Soul

1.Christ-like, see Chapter 1 note for explanation.

2.Hesse, Herman, translated by Hilda Rosner, *Siddhartha*, (New York: Bantam Book, 1980).

Chapter 7
Four Jewels for the Emotional Liberation of the Soul

1. Delaney, John J, *The Practice of the Presence of God by Brother Lawrence of the Resurrection* (New York: Doubleday & Company, 1977).

Suggested Reading

Allen, James, *As a Man Thinketh,* New York: Penguin Group, 1902, 2008, 2011.

Barrick, Marilyn, C., *Emotions: Transforming Anger, Fear and Pain*, Corwin Springs, MT: Summit University Press, 2002.

Booth, Annice, *The Path to Your Ascension: Rediscovering Life's Ultimate Purpose*, Corwin Springs, MT: Summit University Press, 1999.

Byrom, Thomas, *Dhammapada: The Sayings of the Buddha*, Boston, MA: Shambhala Publications, 1993.

Chodron, Pema, *The Places that Scare You: A Guide to Fearlessness in Difficult Times*, Boston, MA: Shambhala, 2001.

Chopich, Erika, and Margaret Paul, *Healing Your Aloneness: Finding Love and Wholeness through Your Inner Child*, New York: HarperCollins, 1990.

Delaney, John J., *The Practice of the Presence of God by Brother Lawrence of the Resurrection*. New York: Doubleday & Company, 1977.

Fillmore, Charles, *The Twelve Powers of Man*, Unity Village, MO: Unity Books, 1930.

Goldsmith, Joel S., *Joel Goldsmith's Gift of Love*, San Francisco, CA: Harper & Row, 1975, 1992.

Goldsmith, Joel S., *Living the Infinite Way*. New York: HarperCollins, 1961.

Goleman, Daniel, with a Scientific Dialogue with Dalai Lama, *Destructive Emotions: How Can We Overcome Them?* New York: Bantam Book, 2003, 2004.

Hanson, Robert, Ph.D., with Richard Mendius, Ph.D., *The Practical Neuroscience of Buddha's Brain: Happiness, Love and Wisdom*. Oakland, CA: New Harbinger. 2009.

Hart, William, *The Art of Living, Vipassana Meditation as Taught by S. N. Goenka*. San Francisco, CA: Harper & Row, 1986.

Hay, Louise, L., *You Can Heal Your Life*, New York: Hay House, 1984, 1987, 2004.

Hendricks, G. & Ludeman, K., *The Mystic Corporate: A Guidebook for Visionaries with their Feet on the Ground*. New York: Bantam Books, 1995.

Hesse, Herman, translated by Hilda Rosner, *Siddhartha*, New York: Bantam Book, 1980.

John of the Cross, Saint, translated and edited by E. Allison Peers, *Dark Night of the Soul,* Garden City, N.Y: Doubleday and Company, 1959.

Kaplan, Aryeh, *Meditation and Kabbalah*, York Beach, ME: Samuel Weiser, 1985.

Kempis, Thomas, translated by John Rooney, *The Imitation of Christ*, Templegate Publishers, 1980.

King, Godfre Ray, *The I AM Discourses (Vol. III)*, Schaumburg, IL: Saint Germain Press, Inc., 1974, 1998.

King, Godfre Ray, *The Magic Presence (Vol. II),* Schaumburg, IL: Saint Germain Press, Inc., 1974, 1982.

King, Godfre Ray, *Unveiled Mysteries (Vol. I)*, Schaumburg, IL: Saint Germain Press, Inc., 1974, 1982.

Kornfield, J., *Art of Forgiveness, Loving- Kindness and Peace*, New York, NY: Bantam Book, 2002, 2004.

Kornfield, J., *Meditation for Beginners: Six Guided Meditations for Inner Clarity and Cultivating a Compassionate Heart*, Boulder Co: Sounds True, 2004, 2008.

Myss, Caroline, Ph.D., *Anatomy of the Spirit: The Seven Stages of Power and Healing*. New York: Harmony Books, 1996.

Neville, *Your Faith is Your Fortune*, Marina del Rey, CA: DeVorss & Company, 1941, 1993, 2011.

Paul, Margaret, Ph.D., *Do I Have to Give Up Me to Be Loved by God?* Deerfield Beach, FL: Health Communications, Inc., 1999.

Paul, Margaret, Ph.D., *Inner Bonding: Becoming a Loving Adult to Your Inner Child*, New York: Harper San Francisco, 1992.

Ponders, Catherine, *The Healing Secret of the Ages*, West Nyack, NY: Parker Publishing, 1973, 1977.

Ponder, Catherine, *The Prospering Power of Love*, Marina del Ray, CA: DeVorss & Company, 1966, 1983.

Prophet, Elizabeth, C., *Quietly Comes the Buddha: Awakening Your Inner Buddha-Nature*, Corwin Springs, MT: Summit University Press, 1998.

Prophet, Mark, L., and Elizabeth Clare Prophet, *Climb the Highest Mountain* (Book One): The Path of the Higher Self, Colorado Springs, CO: Summit Lighthouse, 1972, 1977, 1986.

Prophet, Mark, L., and Elizabeth Clare Prophet, *The Lost Teachings of Jesus 2: Mysteries of the Higher Self*, Livingston, MT: Summit University Press, 1986, 1988.

Prophet, Mark, L., and Elizabeth Clare Prophet, *The Science of the Spoken Word*, Malibu, CA: Summit University Press, 1984.

Sanford, John A., *The Invisible Partners: How the Male and Female in Each of Us Affects our Relationships*. Mahwah, NJ: Paulist Press, 1980.

Stone, Michael, *Freeing the Body, Freeing the Mind: Writings on the Connection Between Yoga and Buddhism*, Boston, MA: Shambhla Publications, Inc., 2010.

Vanzant, Iyanla, *One Day My Soul Just Opened Up*, New York: Simon and Schuster (Fireside), 1999.

Walsch, Neal Donald, *Conversations with God (Book 1)*, New York: G. P. Putman's Sons, 1996.

Yogananada, Paramahansa, *Autobiography of a Yogi*, Los Angeles, CA: Self-Realization Fellowship, 1974, 1983.

Zukav, Gary, *The Seat of the Soul*, New York: Simon & Schuster (Fireside), 1990.

About the Author

With the gifts of curiosity, persistence and spiritual hunger, Dr. Judith Holder's feet were set on the spiritual path early in her life to find the inner and outer dimensions of God. Her parent's library was no ordinary library. It was filled with spiritual books on a wide array of topics that she first attempted to read at the tender age of seven. Even though the words were complex, ethereal, and her comprehension limited by age, her interest and curiosity was larger than life. There was an inner urge to learn, prepare and be ready. She wasn't sure what all this meant at the time, but it kept her searching for deeper meaning and greater spiritual understanding.

When Judith turned 11, her father gave her *Your Faith is Your Fortune* by Neville, which further piqued her interest in the author's perspective on belief, attention, intention and how to realize God through a conscious oneness with universal laws. It captivated her. There were other books along her life's journey—such as *The Practice of the Presence of God* by John Delaney; *The Imitation of Christ* by Thomas a Kempis; *The Prospering Power of Love* by Catherine Ponder, and *Living the Infinite Way* by Joel Goldsmith—that influenced her thinking and began shaping her thoughts and philosophy about soul evolution and life's purpose.

In Judith's early 20s, during college, she took an elective humanities class titled "Man without Boundaries." The professor required students to read books such as *Climb the Highest Mountain* and *The Science of the Spoken Word* by Mark and Elizabeth Prophet, *Siddhartha* by Hermann Hesse, and many other books that covered Eastern and Western religions and philosophies. She was fascinated. It fed the part of her nature, her soul, which felt perpetually hungry for more spiritual substance.

It was during this period that Judith's father, who loved finding mystical, timeworn books from bookstores, came home with two books: *The I AM Discourses* and *The Magic Presence* by Godfre Ray King. Judith quickly devoured both books. Her soul sang with excitement and appreciation to learn more about things that were not spoken of so readily in her daily life. Dr. Holder felt she was on a journey to uncovering the spiritual meaning and reason for her life. She became involved in yoga, Vipassana meditation, and healthy dietary living and pondered why we do what we do in our lives and the soul's psycho-spiritual-emotional educative process. She continues to contemplate these areas to the present day.

Other than her family, she did not encounter many people seeking the meaning of life and how to gracefully pass the initiations and challenges in life. Spirituality was not something people discussed in college or at work. Regardless, Judith remained obedient to her inner self and continued on her path of learning, gathering experiences and listening to her soul promptings.

She became quietly passionate about the interface between psychology and spirituality in daily living, which she refers to as *soul mindfulness psychology*. Her spiritual passion has become an undergarment within her professional attire, insulating and anchoring her as she moves through life and focuses on achieving her professional goals.

Dr. Holder majored in psychology with a minor in community psychology from Montclair State University in New Jersey, received a master's degree in Marriage and Family Therapy and Community Development from the University of Maryland at College Park in Maryland, and later received her doctorate degree in Counseling Psychology with an emphasis in Stress Management from Southern Illinois University at Carbondale in Illinois.

As a former American Psychological Association and National Institute of Occupational Safety and Health fellow at Duke University Medical Center in North Carolina, Dr. Holder is one of the few psychologists clinically trained as an Occupational Health Psychologist in the United States. She received advanced training in business-, executive-, leadership-, career-, performance-, physician-healthcare-, and life-coaching from UNC Charlotte Business Coaching Program™, CoachU™,

MentorCoach™, FastTrack Coaching Program™ and Physician Coaching Institute™. Dr. Holder's greatest joy is coaching, through a collaborative process, clients to achieve their unique personal and professional goals in life and at work. Subsequently, the honing of her clinical skills over the past 27 years along with her educational background and personal evolution has provided a sophisticated array of real-world experiences, skills and abilities she puts to great use in coaching, counseling and in consultation with clients and organizations.

Dr. Holder has had the pleasure of working with clients from many walks of life and with a wide-range of presenting problems. Over the years, there have been curious clients seeking a spiritual pathway. Their questions and hopes of learning how to integrate mind, emotions, and physical drives with soul-spirit understanding have become Dr. Holder's life's mission. This inspires deep thought and the opportunities to ponder how each soul's presenting problem, belief system and emotional reactions ripple, like a pebble in a lake affecting other parts of their life, which either adds or subtracts from attunement to their soul need(s).

Dr. Holder is the founder and executive director of *Uniquely U Pathways: Inspiring You to Be Your Best™ (www.uupathways.com)* dedicated to providing coaching and consulting services. She collaborates with executives, physicians, leaders, professionals, public figures, and people from all walks of life to support them in realizing their life and work aspirations and... soul resilience.

For those interested in *soul mindfulness coaching*™, Dr. Holder collaborates with individuals in exploring how they can maintain a connection to their soul self while moving through life events, such as managing career and life transitions (i.e., loss or grief), work stress and other stressful events, parental concerns, retirement issues, self-esteem and interpersonal dynamics at work and home. Judith's interest is in the interface between these types of life situations and how to support your soul evolution to live a more enriched life. Personally, integrating *soul mindfulness principles* into Dr. Holder's life, and learning from her everyday adventures, is an ongoing life-long evolution. The fun part is we all are walking that same journey together.

Corporate Mystic

"Master," said the student, "where do you get your spiritual power."

"From being connected to the source," said the Master.

"You are connected to the source of Zen?"

"Beyond that," said the Master, "I am Zen. The connection is complete."

"But isn't it arrogant to claim connection with the source?" asked the student.

"Far from it," said the Master. "It's arrogant not to claim connection with the source. Everything is connected. If you think you are not connected to the source you are thumbing your nose at the universe itself."

Hendricks, G. & Ludeman, K. *The Mystic Corporate: A Guidebook for Visionaries with their Feet on the Ground*. New York: Bantam Books, 1995, p. 23.

Ordering Additional and Bulk Copies
Mastering Life's Adventures: On the Beam

Visit book website at
http://www.masteringlifesadventures.com

Note: Free wheel charts can be downloaded from
the book website.

I would enjoy hearing from you ~
leave a comment on the website or
written comments can be mailed to:

Dr. Judith C. Holder
Uniquely U Pathways™/MLA
P.O. Box 13214
Research Triangle Park, NC 27709

~ ~ ~ ~ ~

Visit Dr. Holder's website at:
http://www.uupathways.com
for executive, physician, and leadership coaching and
consulting. She also provides customized workshops
and retreats on various topics to meet your needs as a
small group or organization.

CPSIA information can be obtained at www.ICGtesting.com
Printed in the USA
BVOW021411050712

294392BV00001B/12/P

9 781614 345053